PAUL'S LETTERS
TO THE
EARLY CHURCH

Christian Living Bible Study Series

by Trina Bresser Matous

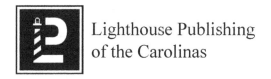
Lighthouse Publishing
of the Carolinas

PRAISE FOR *PAUL'S LETTERS TO THE EARLY CHURCH*

In her book, "Paul's Letters to the Early Church," Trina Bresser Matous gives further clarity to Paul's writings. Trina helps the reader understand the complex early church with a historical and practical application. Trina also challenges the reader with relevant questions pertaining to our own modern day walk with Christ. This is a great read for Biblical scholars and for those who desire to deepen their understanding of Paul's letters.

Jane Jenkins Herlong, CSP
Speaker and Author

When we challenged our congregation with an ambitious Bible reading plan (The Life Journal), Trina was asked to write a refresher commentary to help guide those looking to more accurately understand the Biblical text as they read. Her work exceeded our expectations. Trina's thoughtful insights into both the Old and New Testaments ministered to hundreds of our members every week as the reading plan unfolded. Our congregants snapped her study material off our church shelves every week. I am thrilled that this same resource is now available to a wider audience. Readers will be blessed!

Bryan Hochhalter
Lead Pastor, Grace Community Church (March 2014)

In a world where so many feel that truth is up for grabs, knowing God's word and its background is critical in helping us live lives that reflect His glory. Trina Bresser Matous does a phenomenal job of researching the background of the Bible and pulling out insights that are applicable to life. This volume would be a blessing for any who want to not only know the Bible, but know how to apply the Bible to his or her life.

Wayne Stapleton
Pastor, Renewal Church

Nearly a decade ago our church launched a comprehensive effort to encourage Bible reading in our congregation. In an effort to bring the readings to life, promote discussion and application within the body, Trina Bresser Matous invested full time efforts reading ahead and creating overview notes of the upcoming weeks' readings. Her thorough research, summary and application notes were a huge catalyst to our body's daily engagement with the Scriptures. Over a number of years her work was updated and perfected. We are thrilled that this tool has now become bound in an easy to use series that can be enjoyed by the larger body of Christ. You will find using these supplements, in conjunction with your own Bible reading and study, an enormous encouragement.

Bryce Gray
Elder, Grace Community Church

The depth to which Trina poured her heart into conveying clarity and understanding was only matched by the accuracy of the details given. As an active participant within a church-wide Bible study, I found this resource to be comprehensive, honest and a passionate harvesting of the WORD of God.

Trina's account and interpretation of each book is more than background research, and more than fragmented expositions culled from other commentators. It is a compelling, Spirit led study guide and companion tool. If you are in search of an easy to follow, well outlined approach to studying that remains faithful to the truth of God's Word, look no further!

Dr. Zora Smith Denson
Educational Consultant

PAUL'S LETTERS TO THE EARLY CHURCH BY TRINA BRESSER MATOUS
Published by Lighthouse Publishing of the Carolinas
2333 Barton Oaks Dr., Raleigh, NC, 27614

ISBN 978-1-941103-42-5
Copyright © 2014 by Trina Bresser Matous
Cover design by writelydesigned.com
Interior design by Karthick Srinivasan

Available in print from your local bookstore, online, or from the publisher at:
www.lighthousepublishingofthecarolinas.com

Follow the author online at: @TBresserMatous or facebook.com/TBresserMatous

Brought to you by the creative team at LighthousePublishingoftheCarolinas.com:
Eddie Jones, Barbara King.

Library of Congress Cataloging-in-Publication Data
Bresser Matous, Trina
Paul's Letters To The Early Church/Trina Bresser Matous 1st ed.

Printed in the United States of America

TABLE OF CONTENTS

PHILEMON

HEBREWS

Dedication

To my husband, **Phil**

Thank you for being a godly man who loves and cherishes his wife beyond anything she could have imagined!!

Introduction

Paul's life changed dramatically after his encounter with Jesus Christ. He spent the rest of His life traveling through the Roman Empire sharing the joy and freedom he received when he finally understood Jesus was the Messiah the Jewish people had waited so long for. During his ministry, Paul wrote letters to churches he had planted and hoped to visit, as well as to men he counted as spiritual sons and brothers. Through those letters, Paul detailed many aspects of the theology that defines the Christian faith.

By studying and learning from Paul's letters, believers in the twenty-first century will learn, among other things, how to live peaceably with fellow believers, gain a new appreciation for the hardships of life when viewed against the backdrop of Christ's own suffering, and treasure the deep, abiding joy found by heirs of the Kingdom of God.

Reading and studying Paul's letters can be a daunting task. Verses often require a great deal of study, prayer, and meditation in order to gain an adequate understanding. But don't lose heart! God reveals His Word to those who earnestly seek Him (Jer. 29:13). *Paul's Letters to the Early Church* is designed to assist you in your relationship with God, help you understand difficult passages, shed new light on familiar verses, and gain an appreciation for statements made within the confines of ancient cultural practices. You will learn about Paul and his intense desire to see both Jews and Gentiles not only know about the work of his Savior, Jesus Christ, but also personally experience the love, grace, mercy, and redemption offered by the Father through the sacrifice of the Son. As you learn more about the history and purpose of each verse, you will find yourself growing in wisdom and knowledge.

Though the author of Hebrews is not known with any certainty, it is included with *Paul's Letters to the Early Church* because of its similarity in style and message to the letters known to be written by Paul.

How to use this book

The information given on the following pages should be read in conjunction with the Biblical text. I recommend you read the Biblical text first, then read the associated comments. As you do, ask the Holy Spirit for wisdom and insight.

I have attempted to make the information presented here non-translation specific. You may find, however, that a particular word being discussed does not appear in the translation you are using. The concept still applies. If you want to find the specific word being discussed try looking at different translations, which are easily accessible online.

God's Word has many purposes. He uses it to communicate His great love for and mercy toward all of humanity. He also uses it to speak into our lives. For unbelievers God uses His Word to draw them into faith. For newer believers He uses it to inform and grow their faith. For all believers, God uses His Word to mold and shape us more and more into the image of His Son. James reminded his readers that simply hearing God's Word was not enough; they needed to do it as well (Jam. 1.22). Questions at the end of each chapter are intended to be a catalyst for applying the Biblical text to our lives and experiences in the 21st century. I encourage you to seek and be open to the leading of the Holy Spirit. Spend time thinking about your responses, while being sensitive to promptings of the Holy Spirit to change attitudes, behaviors, or thought patterns.

Use in a small group setting

God uses other believers as well as His Word in our lives. Discussing the chapter-end questions in a small group setting can be beneficial. Other believers' viewpoints and insights can enhance our own understanding of the Biblical text in ways we may not gain on our own. They can also aid our understanding of and response to the trials, hardships, and difficulties we face in our lives. God tells us that we "sharpen" each other as we relate together over His word and what He is doing in our lives. (Prov. 27:17)

God's Word is called the Living Word because God continually reveals new insights. Your insights from a passage may be different than a friend's. This is okay!

Don't be discouraged if your knowledge of the Bible and understanding of the text does not seem as comprehensive as someone else's. God is pleased with anyone who opens His Word and will reveal Himself through it.

Do be encouraged that as you continue to read, pieces will fit together, new understandings will surface and revelations will emerge.

Remember that God is gracious and merciful. He wants a relationship with you through His Son, Jesus Christ. So take a breath, enjoy His Word, and come to know Him better.

Enjoy your journey with God. His Word is rich and will add meaning to your life!

GALATIANS

Paul wrote his letter to the Galatians to combat a specific false teaching that was beginning to make inroads with the believers in Galatia. The heresy was addressed in a clear, direct and concise manner that would have left Paul's readers with little doubt about where Paul stood on the issue. He used a persuasive method common to ancient speakers and writers that was designed to motivate people to change their behavior.

The false teaching being preached in Galatia required Gentile Christians to observe Jewish practices, primarily circumcision, in order to enter fully into God's family. This directly opposed Paul's teaching that adoption into God's family was achieved simply by believing the message of the cross of Christ. No other work was required.

Paul is believed to have written this letter between 48 and 52 A.D. If these dates are correct, Galatians was the first or close to the first letter Paul wrote. This would also make it one of the oldest New Testament writings.

In many ways, the letter to the Galatians is a standard first century letter and contains typical elements of such writings: introduction (1.1-5), body (1.6-6.10) and conclusion (6.11-18). Absent are elements contained in Paul's other letters, including an introductory thanksgiving statement and concluding greetings. The absence of these elements may point to the critical nature of the issue in Paul's eyes.

Galatians can be divided into three parts. The first, chapters 1-2, focuses on Paul's authority as an apostle and the gospel message he preached. The second, chapters 3-4, is more doctrinal in nature and defends salvation by faith alone while criticizing the bondage that accompanies legalism. The final part, chapters 5-6, is more practical in nature as Paul exhorted the Galatians to live out the freedom of the gospel in love of and service to those around them.

Galatians, Chapter 1

BACKGROUND

Paul's first missionary journey took him through Phrygia in southern Galatia while his second journey took him through northern Galatia (modern day central Turkey). Paul addressed his letter to *the churches of Galatia*. Galatia could be used as either an ethnic or a political reference. Technically, Galatia referred to North Galatia, but its ethnic connotations could have referred to the Phrygia region. As a result, scholars have debated whether Paul used the term in an ethnic or geopolitical nature.[1]

OVERVIEW

It was customary to open with the sender's name, though less so to include a description of the sender in the opening statement.

Paul's claim to apostleship was the result of his Damascus Road conversion (Acts 9.1-20).

It was customary to include a word of thanksgiving in the opening part of a letter. Paul, however, skipped this convention and moved right to his rebuke. Such a practice was reserved only for the harshest of letters.

The Greek translated as *I marvel* or *I am amazed* would have left Paul's readers with little doubt that he was irritated. His irritation stemmed from an errant gospel that was being preached by false teachers and believed by the members of the churches in Galatia. The Galatians had

---

[1] Craig S. Keener, The IVP Bible Background Commentary: New Testament (Accordance electronic ed. Downers Grove: InterVarsity Press, 1993)

heard the true gospel message from Paul. Any deviation from what he had taught was a perversion of the gospel and the false teacher should stand accused (condemned). So adamant was Paul about the purity of the gospel message that he repeated his assertion that those teaching the false gospel should be eternally condemned.

As a servant of Jesus Christ, Paul was not concerned about pleasing men but only about doing that which pleased God.

Paul included an autobiographical section that runs from 1.11 through 2.13. It is one of the longest such sections in Paul's letters.

First hand knowledge was highly valued in Jewish culture. Paul claimed that the gospel he preached had been received directly from God through the revelation of Jesus.

Advancing was a technical term meaning progressing in one's studies.

Paul's call by God was similar to Jeremiah's (Jer. 1.5).

Some translations use *flesh and blood* to indicate mortals; other translations use *any man*.

Paul had previously tried to earn his salvation, just as the Judaizers were attempting to do. Through his conversion experience, Paul learned that salvation came through the grace of God alone, not by his works.

Paul's conversion was followed by time in Arabia, the area near Damascus in Syria. Only then did he go to Jerusalem where he had an opportunity to spend time with Peter. After which he visited Syria (Antioch) and Cilicia (Tarsus).

One of the greatest testimonies to newfound faith in Christ is a life that has been changed for the better. Paul had once been zealous to destroy the faith but now worked even more zealously to advance it.

INSIGHTS

Paul and Jeremiah were not unique when it came to God knowing them and putting a call on their lives before they were born. God knows each of us intimately long before we are born. For those who eventually choose to place their faith in Christ, God also gives each a call or purpose that will serve to advance His kingdom to the ends of the earth. Some people quickly embrace God's call in their lives while others may spend years fighting before eventually conceding to God's desires. However each of us arrives at embracing God's call on our lives, there is nothing more fulfilling than doing what God designed us to do.

1. Paul was concerned the believers in Galatia were turning away from the good news of Christ to believe a false gospel. How can we ensure we do not fall into a similar trap of believing false statements about Christ and the gospel?

2. Paul guarded against seeking to please men, focusing instead on fulfilling his calling by Christ. In what ways do we seek to please men instead of God? Are there areas in your life where God wants you to place more focus on His calling for your life?

GALATIANS, CHAPTER 2

BACKGROUND

Depending on when the letter to the Galatians was written, Paul's journey to Jerusalem, as mentioned in Galatians 2, corresponds to either Acts 11.27-30 or Acts 15.2.

Though not mentioned in Acts, Titus responded to Paul's gospel message and became a believer (Tit. 1.4). Titus seems to have been an effective ministry partner over a number of years (2 Cor. 8.23).

OVERVIEW

Prior to the life of Christ, most Jews believed a Gentile could convert to Judaism but were not on equal terms with the Jewish community until they were circumcised. It is, therefore, not surprising that some Jewish Christians wanted Titus to be circumcised. The agreement of the Jerusalem Council that circumcision was not required for Gentile believers was a significant departure from the majority view.

Paul used strong language to identify those who believed circumcision was necessary: false brothers engaged in spying who sought to imprison true believers. The true gospel message that Paul preached had never given way to the teachings of the false brothers.

Paul pointed out that the *pillars* of the faith, James, Peter and John, were not superior to him in their understanding of the gospel and in fact concurred with his own understanding.

Paul and Peter were not called to preach two different gospel messages but the same. The only difference was that Paul was called to the Gentile community, while Peter was sent to the Jewish community.

In Paul's view, Peter's refusal to eat with Gentiles while in Antioch was hypocritical and contradictory to the decision made by the council in Jerusalem. Withdrawing from table fellowship with Gentiles threatened the unity of the church and made the Gentile believers out to be second-class citizens. Since Peter's reputation caused many others including Barnabas to follow his example, Paul felt he had no choice but to confront Peter publicly on the issue.

It is unclear whether verses 15-21 represent a continuation of Paul's confrontation with Peter or serve as a thesis for the entire letter.

Paul recognized that Jews were sinners just as Gentiles were. However, the Jewish people had the spiritual advantage of knowing how to be justified before God. That justification was not the result of keeping the Law of Moses, performing good deeds, or doing any other type of work. Rather, justification (salvation) comes only through faith in Jesus Christ by the grace of God.

Paul rejected the idea that if one continued to sin after placing his/her faith in Christ then Jesus would be a promoter of sin. Those who might attempt to assert the law as playing a part in justification were convicted as transgressors by the law itself. The law was not sinful. It served to point people to their own spiritual barrenness and need for God's grace through Jesus Christ.

Paul concluded by stating that he shared in the crucifixion of Christ and in doing so, it was no longer Paul who lived but the resurrected Jesus who lived in him. If righteousness were obtainable through the law, then Christ's death was meaningless.

INSIGHTS

Paul argued strongly and convincingly that salvation resulted from faith in Jesus Christ alone. No other work of any kind was required.

Nor did such salvation depend in any manner on the degree to which one had avoided sin. *Great* sin and *little* sin were forgiven when one placed one's trust in Christ. Some people today are hindered from the salvation Christ offers because they believe God could never forgive the sin they have committed. This is simply not true. Salvation is available to *all people* simply by believing in Christ and receiving the forgiveness God freely offers.

1. Paul confronted Peter for being hypocritical and sowing seeds of disunity among believers. What practices and attitudes do we have that contribute to conflict and dissention among believers today?

2. What areas of your life do you need to surrender to Christ so that with Paul you might say, "It is no longer I who live, but Christ who lives in me"?

3. Is there any past sin you are holding onto because you believe God could never forgive you for it? How can you release it to God and accept the forgiveness He freely offers, that it may no longer be a barrier between you and God?

GALATIANS, CHAPTER 3

BACKGROUND

Paul's knowledge of scripture was thorough and he used it well to state his case. In this chapter, he used the only two references (Gen. 15.6 and Hab. 2.4) in the entire Old Testament that speak of righteousness and faith together in order to drive home his point.

OVERVIEW

Paul's question was designed to point out that the empowerment or indwelling of the Holy Spirit came as a result of faith, not because of adherence to the law. What came by faith was not later maintained by keeping the law.

Paul appealed to the ultimate eyewitness confirmation: the experience of the listeners themselves. What was the meaning of the persecution they suffered after coming to faith? Did it count for something or was it suffered for no reason?

The Judaizers were likely pointing to Abraham to show that circumcision was necessary. Paul quoted from the same scriptures the Judaizers likely used in order to show that Abraham was justified by faith alone (Gen. 15.6).

All who had faith were spiritual *sons of Abraham* regardless of whether they were Jews or Gentiles. God's plan had always included the Gentiles as was evident by His promise that Abraham would be a blessing to *all the nations* (Gen 18.18).

Anyone who did not keep (confirm) the whole law was cursed

(Deut. 27.26). Paul argued that everyone was therefore cursed because it was impossible for anyone to keep the entire law perfectly.

Paul quoted Habakkuk 2.4 as further evidence that nothing more than faith was required to be justified.

Having established the insufficiency of the law, Paul reiterated his main point: Jesus had taken on the curse of all who could not keep the law, so that they in turn might be justified through faith in Him.

God's covenant with His people was fulfilled in Christ. All Jews were considered the physical seed of Abraham, but Jesus was the final focus of God's promise and was therefore the ultimate Seed.

Israel was in Egypt for four hundred and thirty years. The law was given to the people at the end of this period but was at odds with the promise God made to Abraham. Any attempt to prove that the law was a fulfillment of that promise had no spiritual basis.

The law served as an intermediary step between God's promise to Abraham and the fulfillment of that promise through Jesus (the Seed). The law was given through a mediator, Moses, but God alone consummated the promise made with Abraham.

A tutor would offer instruction and correction to the children under his care. The law served a similar role by providing instruction and correction until the time of Christ was revealed, after which time the tutorage of the law would no longer be needed.

By *putting on Christ* through conversion, Gentiles took their place as Abraham's seed (heirs). More importantly, there was no longer any ethnic or social distinction between believers; all were equal in Christ.

INSIGHTS

Paul's teaching that *there is neither Jew nor Greek, there is neither slave nor free, there is neither male nor female; for you are all one in Christ Jesus* is worth heeding today. It can be far too easy to judge others as better or worse than we are—to categorize others in ways God never intended.

If the others are believers, Jesus leveled the playing field and we are all equal. If they are not believers, God desires to call them sons and daughters, so we do well to treat them with the love of Christ, thereby encouraging them to realize the saving grace of Jesus for themselves.

1. Paul passionately and skillfully argued that the law was not the means to obtain salvation, which came from faith in Christ alone. Are there any ways in which you are attempting to earn your salvation by keeping a set of rules, striving to reach a particular standard or seeking to rise to a certain level of competence?

2. Though the Jews had a long history of being God's chosen people, Paul was adamant that salvation through faith in Christ was available equally to the Gentiles and the Jews; a radical thought in Paul's day. Are there people we judge as unworthy of being saved? If so, do you think Paul would agree with your argument if you could make it to him today?

GALATIANS, CHAPTER 4

BACKGROUND

The physical infirmity from which Paul suffered is unknown. It may have been an illness contracted on his way to Galatia (malaria was known to be common in the area) or the ailment from which he prayed for healing and from which God chose not to heal him (2 Cor. 12.7-10). Some have speculated that Paul's ailment may have been near blindness, which would explain the reference to *your eyes* as well as the apparent size of his handwriting (6.11).

OVERVIEW

Paul built on the idea of tutors and heirs by exploring the meaning of adopted sons.

According to Roman law, the status of a minor was roughly the same as that of a slave. A child had to wait until the time appointed by his father to inherit what was to be his. In Paul's view, this was similar to what God had done by giving the law and delaying Jesus' coming. The bondage of the world had been a common experience. God had given the law as a guide and in the fullness of time (the time appointed or chosen by God) sent His Son so that those under the law might be received as the adopted sons (and daughters!) of God.

Because Jesus was *born of a woman* He was fully human; because He was *born under the law* He was subject to the same Jewish law as the rest of God's called people. This also further established Jesus' identification with those subject to the law.

The Spirit was sent to all believers in the same fullness of time that God's Son was sent. The indwelling of the Spirit allows each to have an intimate relationship with the Father and receive full inheritance as a son.

Though the Galatians had experienced freedom from bondage through their faith in Christ, they were turning back to the elements that had put them in bondage in the first place.

Paul feared that the effort he had put into preaching the good news to the Galatians would prove to be wasted time.

Paul turned to the bond of friendship that had developed with the Galatians during his visit.

Zealousness was good if it was based on a good thing, but the zealousness being displayed for the Galatians was founded on error.

Paul related to the Galatians as both their spiritual father (*my little children*, so called because of their lack of spiritual growth and maturity) and spiritual mother (*labor pains*, which Paul was experiencing again because of their fall into erroneous thinking).

Paul concluded his argument by referring to Abraham's two sons. Hagar, a bondwoman (servant), conceived the first, while Sarah, Abraham's legitimate wife, conceived the second (Gen. 16; 21). Paul's contrast of the sons was allegorical to the contrast between the covenants that were at odds with each other in Galatia: the promise made to Abraham (Gen. 12.1-3) vs. the Law of Moses given at Mt. Sinai (Ex. 19-23).

In a similar contrast, Paul spoke of the Jerusalem now, which related to the Law, and the Jerusalem to come, which represented the hope of God's coming kingdom.

Paul quoted Isaiah 54.1 to demonstrate that the children of promise would far outweigh those of the judgment and exile.

Just as Hagar and Ishmael were eventually cast out (Gen. 21.9-12) because Ishmael was not the son of promise, so the Galatians needed to cast out the message of bondage and return to the hope of the good news of Christ.

INSIGHTS

Paul repeatedly quoted from the Hebrew Scriptures (our Old Testament) as he presented his argument to the Galatians. His ability to do so came from thorough knowledge and understanding of the scriptures. Following Paul's example by taking time to study the scriptures will serve to grow our own faith and understanding of the redemption God offers to all humanity as well as prepare us to defend the hope we have in Christ (1 Pet. 3.15). Though many believe they can never know the scriptures as well as their pastor or other learned friend, time spent studying the scripture is never wasted and always pays off.

1. Paul told his readers that in the fullness of time God sent forth His Son to redeem those under the law that we might be released from the bondage of the law. What does it mean to live free of bondage? Once freed from bondage, how do we sometimes choose to return to bondage? In what areas are we choosing to live in bondage, despite the freedom offered through faith in Christ?

2. As believers in Jesus Christ, we have been empowered by the Holy Spirit and are heirs of God. How do we fully live out this truth?

BACKGROUND

Uncertainty exists about which spirit Paul referred to in his discussion of a person's life in Christ. The reference could have been to the Holy *Spirit* or to the human *spirit*. God's work is in the human spirit by the Holy Spirit to move people away from sin and toward Christian virtues. The ultimate goal is that each person is crucified to the desires of the flesh and produces the fruits of the Spirit. Whichever way *spirit* is understood, Paul's exhortation does not change.

OVERVIEW

Paul concluded this section of his argument by encouraging the Galatians to stand on the freedom available in Christ and not to take on the bondage of slavery again.

The problem with circumcision was that it turned the believer away from God's grace and towards one's own abilities. Anyone who did choose to be circumcised became obligated to keep the law and alienated from Christ. Such alienation meant that Christ's death and resurrection had no value.

God's promised kingdom began with the life of Christ but has not been fully realized on earth. As a result, the Spirit activated the power of the future kingdom in the present for believers. Believers are thus able to enjoy the righteousness that will be fully realized upon Christ's return.

Only a small amount of yeast (leaven) is needed as it works its way through the entire loaf. In the same way, the perversion being taught by the false teachers could spread through the whole community if not checked.

The persecution Paul suffered attested to the gospel of grace he preached. It is likely that Paul's decision to have Timothy circumcised (Acts 16.3) had been misconstrued. Paul could not be preaching both circumcision and the cross because they were contradictory to each other.

The freedom (liberty) found in Christ could tempt one in the opposite direction, resulting in legalism. In this scenario, one could be tempted to justify any behavior at all. True freedom in Christ was evidenced by one's desire to serve others in love.

The lusts of the flesh are the sinful desires inherent in each person. The only way to overcome succumbing to those desires is by walking in the power of the Holy Spirit.

Lists of vices were common in ancient writings on morality. Pagan writers emphasized the need to avoid excess in most vices while Paul was much more forceful by stating that *all* (indicated by *and the like*) vices should be avoided.

Paul contrasted the works of the flesh with the fruit of the Spirit. Fruit would be a natural outpouring of those made new in Christ.

While ancient philosophers often spoke of human efforts to bring passions under control, Paul pointed to the death of those passions through the spiritual crucifixion one experienced by placing one's faith in Christ. Such death may not be instantaneous and requires a continual turning to Christ for strength. Christ offers victory over such passions that human effort alone can never achieve.

Paul exhorted the Galatians to walk with the Spirit since they were already living by the Spirit. Such a choice would be evidenced by the way they treated one another.

INSIGHTS

Paul's caution that the freedom found in Christ not be misused is as real today as it was in his time. Since we live under grace and God freely forgives sin as we repent of it, some may be tempted to live a life of no constraint and great worldly pleasure. Why not enjoy life for all its worth, they ask, when God so freely forgives. Yet such a life does not reflect God's character, in whose image we were created, and is not pleasing to Him. Such a lifestyle is not without its consequences, most of which are undesirable, and ultimately leads to regret and an absence of the blessings and fulfillment God intends for all who believe in His Son.

1. Are there any areas of your life where you are willfully disobedient to God? Are there any areas you are abusing God's gift of liberty by continuing to sin?

2. Paul listed nine items as fruit of the Holy Spirit, meaning evidence of the Holy Spirit at work in a believer's life. Curiously, Paul used the singular fruit for these nine items indicating all should be evident in a believer fully surrendered to Christ. How is this fruit evident in your life? What do you need to surrender or submit to Christ in order to experience more fully the Holy Spirit's fruit in your life?

GALATIANS, CHAPTER 6

BACKGROUND

Paul prayed that *the Lord Jesus Christ be with your spirit.* Since all are made in the image of God (Gen. 1.26-27), all are comprised of both body and spirit. While the emphasis of Galatians was on a practice performed on the physical body, Paul was equally concerned with each person's spirit. The physical body would die, but the spirit does not die. The eternal existence of the spirit, either life or death, depends on the choice each makes in the physical body to accept or reject Christ.

OVERVIEW

Paul turned his attention to the spiritual restoration of sinners and overburdened brothers.

A believer overtaken (caught off guard) by sin needed to be approached gently. *Consider yourself* could have applied to one of two things: either taking care to not fall into the same temptation the sinful brother had or not to assume an attitude of pride because one had avoided what another had fallen into.

The law of Christ likely referred to the second of the greatest commandments: to love others as you love yourself. Doing so would motivate the believer to help those who had fallen into sin as well as those who were suffering more than they could bear.

The Greek word translated as *burden* referred to something that was beyond the ability of one person to carry. *Load*, on the other hand, referred to that which one could be reasonably expected to carry.

To be *something* meant taking excessive pride in oneself as compared to another. Such a person might think he was something special but in reality was deceiving himself.

In the highly agrarian culture of Paul's time, sowing and reaping would have been quite familiar. No one would have expected to sow one type of seed and reap another type of crop. Paul warned that sowing (living by) the lusts of the flesh (sin) would lead to a *crop* of corruption while sowing (living by) the Holy Spirit would lead to eternal rewards. He also encouraged his readers to continue doing what was right—even when tempted to do otherwise, because an ultimate reward would be waiting for them in heaven.

Many reasons have been suggested as to why Paul wrote with such large letters. Whatever the reason was, Paul wrote the letter, or at least a portion of the letter, himself, instead of employing a scribe as was customary.

Paul once again returned to the theme of circumcision. As he had previously stated, circumcision leads one to live by the law, a mandate that those who taught circumcision could not even keep themselves.

While others would boast in the circumcision they required of others, Paul would boast only in the cross of Christ; it was from that alone that believers became the new creations God desired them to be.

It is unlikely that Paul actually bore the same scars as Jesus had, though his earlier stoning or multiple beatings may have left him with marks that were similar. He had also almost died at one point and may have therefore associated more closely with Christ's own death since both had suffered for the same reason: the good news they preached.

INSIGHTS

Paul instructed his readers not to build themselves up through comparison with others. Such pride was misplaced and not pleasing to God. It is so easy to judge others by saying, "At least I'm not like him" or "*I've* never done what she has done." In so doing we fail to acknowledge our own sinfulness. While human nature tends to categorize sin on a scale of not so bad to horrible, God sees and judges all sin the same. There is no gray in God's eyes. As a result we all stand before God condemned by our own sin. We who have chosen to put our faith in Christ do not suffer the deserved condemnation, but enjoy redemption instead.

1. Paul called the Galatians to bear one another's burden. How is God calling you to walk alongside a spiritual brother or sister or even an unbeliever during their time of trial, suffering or need? In what ways is God asking you to help bear their burdens?

2. Paul was determined to boast only in the cross of Christ, having let the world die to him and him to the world. Do you boast in anything other than Christ? If so, is this an area you need to surrender to Christ?

FIRST CORINTHIANS

Paul visited Corinth on his second missionary journey. During that time he preached the gospel of Christ and established a body of believers. After eighteen months in the city he departed for Jerusalem. Paul maintained contact with the church through correspondence. Two of those letters, 1 and 2 Corinthians, have survived. At least one other letter is known to have been written (1 Cor. 5.9-11), with some scholars believing there were at least four in total.

Corinth was a prosperous and flourishing city at the time of Paul's visit. Its location on the isthmus of what is modern day southern Greece put it on the trade route for ships crossing the Mediterranean Sea, resulting in not only a great exposure to different cultural practices but religions as well. Its prosperity attracted a variety of pleasure-seekers who brought with them many pagan customs. Corinth gained such a notorious reputation that *acting like a Corinthian (korinthiazomai)* became a synonym for sexual immorality and prostitution.

In the midst of such immoral pagan lures, the young Corinthian church was struggling with the decadent culture of the city. Not only were the believers succumbing to the temptations, they were identifying with specific Christian leaders in the community and allowing division to threaten the unity that was to be found in Christ.

Two letters sent to him from Corinth motivated Paul's correspondence. The first came from the household of Chloe (1.11) while the second was a list of questions sent by the believers and likely delivered by Stephanas, Fortunatus, and Achaicus (7.1; 16.15-18).

First Corinthians can be divided into two parts. The first part, chapters 1-6, deals with Paul's rebuke of the sinful behavior into which many in the church had fallen. The second part, chapters 7-16, deals with specific questions presented to Paul by the messengers from the church.

1 Corinthians, Chapter 1

BACKGROUND

The identity of Sosthenes, named in Paul's introduction, is not known with certainty. Some have speculated he was the same synagogue leader who was beaten because of his association with Paul (Acts 18.12-17). Since ancient letters were usually not coauthored, Paul may have wanted to add weight to his message by including the endorsement of a respected community leader.

OVERVIEW

Both *sanctified* and *saints* mean *set apart* or *holy and separated for God*. While this language was specific to Israel in the Old Testament, it encompassed all believers in Christ in New Testament times.

By associating Jesus with God, Paul was pointing to His divinity.

Because Paul was writing concerning problems in the Corinthian church, his thanksgiving (another standard element in many ancient letters) was directed more toward the work God was doing in the believers' lives than for the believers themselves, as he does in some of his other letters (Eph. 1.15-16; Phil. 1.3-5).

Paul was confident that the disgraceful Corinthians would stand blameless before God, not because of their own work but because of the work of Christ in them.

Divisions had developed in the Corinthian church, creating the problem Paul needed to address. Paul pleaded with the believers to set aside their differences and come together in unity of speech (external) as well as be joined together in unity of heart and mind (internal) that they might express the unity of one body in Christ.

Though baptism was a sign of faith in Christ, Paul put minimal emphasis on it, focusing instead on the importance of hearing the message of Christ. Paul didn't want *who* had performed one's baptism to become more important that *what* had occurred, i.e. membership in God's family due to faith in Christ.

Paul expanded the theme of Isaiah 29.14 to show that worldly wisdom would one day come to nothing.

Some tout human wisdom as humanity's best hope. Those people see the wisdom of God, which includes the message of the cross, as foolishness. Yet just the opposite is true. When people understand the message of the cross, they realize it offers what human wisdom can never even dream of offering – salvation and eternal life.

Irony was a common rhetorical device and Paul used it to show that the least of God's wisdom and strength is greater than anything humans can bring forth.

Most Corinthians came from the lower classes and didn't fall into the category of the wise (Greek philosophers), mighty (politically powerful) or noble (assigned by birth rather than wealth).

Divisions in the churches at Corinth had resulted from comparison between humans and God (1.20-25) as well as between the church and rest of the world (1.26-31).

In terms of people, the lowly (base) and despised would have referred to slaves, of which there were many in Corinth. These people would not have been given great value in the world's estimation but enjoyed God's grace through His wisdom.

Paul paraphrased Jeremiah 9.24 as he encouraged his readers to boast in only what was worthy of boasting – the work of Jesus Christ.

INSIGHTS

Just as in Paul's time, the wisdom of the world can be very enticing. Those arguing in its favor can give convincing reasons as to why it is worthy of our time, energy and hope. In contrast, God's wisdom can seem uninspiring, unintelligent and impractical, in short, foolish. Yet the ultimate of ironies is that the world's wisdom leads to the opposite of what it purports: lack of fulfillment, disease, purposelessness, and ultimately death. On the other hand, God's wisdom will give us personal fulfillment and purpose in life, joy, deep satisfaction and the ultimate of benefits – eternal life with God in His heavenly kingdom.

1. Paul pleaded with the Corinthians that there be no divisions between them, but that they live perfectly joined in mind and judgment. Despite the many denominational beliefs today, how can we put Paul's exhortation into practice? Which are matters of faith that we need to stand firm on? Which are denominational preferences in which we can allow for differences?

2. Paul was thankful that Jesus enriched the Corinthians in speech and knowledge. How should we live to enrich our lives continually by the wisdom and grace of Jesus Christ?

1 Corinthians, Chapter 2

BACKGROUND

Paul referred to God's hidden or secret wisdom, which he defined as *revelation . . . hidden for long ages past, but now revealed and made known* (Rom. 16.25-26). The message was known only to God and revealed at His chosen time. A later Gnostic doctrine falsely taught that this mystery was secret knowledge available only to those admitted into the inner circle of the faith.

OVERVIEW

Paul continued his theme of human wisdom vs. God's wisdom. His illustration was his own preaching to the Corinthians. It was not his brilliantly presented persuasive speech that drew the people to faith but the power of God's Spirit working through Paul that lead to their salvation.

By referring to his own weakness, Paul allowed the strength of the gospel message to be plainly visible.

Demonstration of the Spirit's power referred not only to the people who placed their faith in Christ as a result of the good news they heard. It also referred to signs and wonders (healings, miracles and other supernatural works) that often accompanied such preaching.

Human wisdom was no match for the eternal and unfailing wisdom of God.

Rulers of this age (v. 8) referred to the Jewish and Greek leaders who were responsible for Jesus' crucifixion.

Paul paraphrased Isaiah 64.4 to demonstrate that wisdom and knowledge belong to God alone. Because God's Spirit resides in those who believe, they too can know what is in God's heart and act with His wisdom and knowledge. This would have been a radical thought for the people of Paul's time. The Spirit had been active in Old Testament times but generally only in specific individuals to carry out specific mandates. Paul was teaching that the Spirit was active in *all* believers. It is that Spirit that teaches what the believers could not have known solely through human efforts.

The Holy Spirit serves as humanity's teacher and as such reveals spiritual things that cannot be known by any other means. Therefore, human wisdom and effort can never discern what the Spirit reveals.

The natural man is anyone who does not have the Holy Spirit.

The ability of the spiritual person to *judge all things* refers to the discernment one obtains once indwelt with the Holy Spirit. Such a person can determine what is or is not of Christ.

INSIGHTS

Faith in Christ not only gives us benefits in the life to come, namely eternal life, but benefits in this life as well. One of those is the indwelling of the Holy Spirit and the wisdom and discernment that result. Through the Holy Spirit we can have an intimate relationship with God. As we grow in our relationship with God, we also grow in our knowledge of God's heart. We are better able to discern His will and live in a manner that increases our own peace and joy. Even in the midst of trial we can be at rest as God, through His Spirit, continually reassures us.

1. How do we ensure that our faith rests squarely and firmly on the power of God and not the wisdom of men?

2. What does it mean that we have received the Spirit who is from God? What has God freely given through His Spirit that He wants us to know?

1 Corinthians, Chapter 3

BACKGROUND

Paul used the plural form of *you* in Greek when he spoke of being the temple of God (v. 16-17). He was referring to the church, the body of believers, in whom God's Spirit dwelt. This was in contrast to the fragmented and broken humanity of the world. The alternative to that fragmentation and brokenness is the hope that lies in God, which the church, the body of believers, was called to model.

OVERVIEW

Paul did not equate natural and carnal (worldly). The natural person was one who had not received the Spirit of God (2.14). The carnal person had received the Spirit but was still very young in his/her faith.

Just as the maturity of a child did not take place overnight, so Paul had not expected the Corinthian believers to become mature immediately upon hearing the gospel message. Maturity should begin to make itself evident over time but had not with the Corinthian believers. Instead, they were still so young in their faith they were *eating* the milk of babies rather than the solid food of the more mature. The evidence of that lack of maturity was seen in their behavior. It should have been aligning itself with the person of Christ and their righteous position in Him. Their behavior, however, still included envy, strife and other behaviors that caused division.

Paul used an agricultural analogy to make his point. Sowing and watering were both necessary to realize a harvest but it was God who caused the increase or made things grow. The Corinthian believers should not divide themselves among the caretakers but look to the one who called them to Himself.

As Paul continued his point, he switched from an agricultural to a building analogy. Paul had laid the foundation, which was Jesus Christ, while others had built upon it.

Gold, silver, precious stones, wood, hay and straw were building materials of differing qualities.

The day was an Old Testament term for the final day of judgment. Paul used it to refer to Christ's judgment of the work of His servants, not their salvation. Fire also referred to judgment but was not the fire of eternal punishment. Rather it was the fire that purified gold and silver but consumed wood and hay. Anyone whose work was judged worthy would receive a reward. Those whose work was done with consumable materials would suffer loss but would not lose their salvation.

Paul used the word *temple* to refer to the church body. Anyone who did not honor the presence of God's Spirit within the body of the church was at risk of God's discipline. In this sense *God will destroy him* referred to discipline of the individual rather than loss of salvation because of eternal death.

Paul again stated that the wisdom of the world was foolishness to God and what the world saw as the foolishness of God was true wisdom.

Paul quoted from Job 5.13 and Psalm 94.11. Both stress the futility of human wisdom. In quoting these scriptures, Paul was urging the Corinthians to humble themselves before God and seek His wisdom.

Jesus was (is) the source of all things, so boasting in one man over another accomplished nothing.

INSIGHTS

Just as Paul and Apollos planted and watered what became the Corinthian church, so God calls each of us to fulfill a specific part of His plan. No one person is called to do it all and each person's role is just as important as the next. God calls some to have prominent roles in a church or community while others are called to work behind the scenes. Many have come to Christ because the "foundation" was laid by the behind the scenes believer and the "building" was done by the upfront believer. Even the most insignificant act done in obedience to God is not missed and contributes to the rewards God will one day give believers.

1. How can we ensure we are not what Paul calls fleshly but instead are eating the food of spiritual maturity?

2. It can be easy to focus on the preaching and ministry of a particular person. How do we maintain proper perspective that all are servants of God, who alone brings about our growth and maturity in Him?

1 CORINTHIANS, CHAPTER 4

BACKGROUND

Sarcasm was as much an effective rhetorical device in ancient times as it is today. Paul used sarcasm to challenge the status quo. He wanted to cause his readers to not only think about what he had written but cause them to take a close look at themselves. By challenging their assumptions and self-righteousness, Paul hoped to help his readers see the incompatibility of their position with that of Christ's and bring them into better alignment with the hope of Christ.

OVERVIEW

Most slaves were servants, but only the most trustworthy earned the position of steward, a position that held such responsibilities as managing the owner's financial and household affairs. Anyone serving in such a position had to be faithful, i.e. trustworthy.

Paul was not making a case for not being accountable; the constructive criticisms of those around him were of value. Ultimately, however, the only judgment he was concerned with was God's.

The meaning of the phrase *not to go (think) beyond what is written* is unclear. Several possibilities have been suggested: scripture could be used to strengthen the church or it could be misused to exalt oneself and weaken the church; not overstepping the bounds of a written contract; or the scripture verses Paul had previously quoted in his letter.

Paul addressed the pride that was permeating the Corinthian

believers. They boasted about what they had as if it were theirs to boast about. Paul reminded them that, in fact, everything they had was the result of God's generosity.

The Corinthian believers thought that Christ's kingdom in the present included having all they wanted, being rich and reigning as kings. Paul knew trials were part of Christ's kingdom and hoped that they would one day reign together.

Spectacle was a reference to the public executions or games that would exhibit gladiators. Those forced to participate were subjected to torment, wild animal attacks and jeering crowds. In this case, it was God who put the suffering of the apostles on display. Paul went on to compare the lofty opinions the Corinthians had of themselves with the world's opinion of himself. Paul knew that real strength was found in Christ working through his weaknesses.

Paul listed the abuses, both physical and verbal, he had suffered in delivering the message of Jesus. His purpose was not to shame and condemn his readers but to give warning and correction.

Paul pointed to a difference between a teacher and a father. Many could teach, but only one could claim to be the father. In this case, Paul was claiming spiritual fatherhood of the Corinthian believers since he was the first to preach to them and "birth" that body of believers. As such, he had more responsibility for them than their teachers.

Paul asserted he would be able to discern between those who lived conceited, self-righteous lives and those who lived in the present kingdom of God. The latter would allow the power of Christ to reign in their hearts.

As the spiritual father of the Corinthian church, Paul had the authority to administer discipline, though he preferred to come in love and with a spirit of gentleness.

INSIGHTS

Paul could not visit the Corinthian church, so he sent Timothy, his trusted co-worker, in his place. Given the difficulties being exhibited by the Corinthian believers, Paul had to send someone with a well-established, mature faith and understanding of Christ. God desires to use us in important ways to further His kingdom. Just like Timothy, we need to be sure of our faith and the teachings of Christ. Such assurance is not gained overnight but through studying God's Word, living through trials and difficulties, and being intentional about our relationship with God. These do take effort, but the payoff is the blessings of God.

1. What does it mean to be a steward of the mysteries of God?

2. Paul warned his readers to be cautious in light of instruction from many different Christians, to remember the foundations of faith that he, as their spiritual father, had taught them. What foundational, spiritual truths are important for us to remember? How do we risk believing half-truths and lies from well-intentioned people when we forget the foundational truths?

1 Corinthians, Chapter 5

BACKGROUND

Paul used the phrase *do you not know* ten times in 1 Corinthians (3.16; 5.6; 6.2, 3, 9, 15, 16, 19; 9.13, 24). Each time, he used it to introduce an irrefutable statement; something the Corinthians should have known to be true.

When God delivered His people from Egyptian slavery, they left so fast they did not have time to wait for the bread to rise. Succeeding generations commemorated the flight from Egypt with a Passover meal, complete with unleavened bread (bread without yeast; Ex. 12).

OVERVIEW

Paul turned from issues of church unity to issues concerning sexual morality.

The use of the term *his father's wife* is thought to indicate the woman was the offender's stepmother. The focus on the offender likely indicates he was a believer while the woman was not. Church discipline is reserved for believers and does not extend to those who are not believers.

A misunderstanding of God's grace motivated the Corinthians' pride in their tolerance of immoral behavior. The Corinthian believers thought they could enjoy freedom without limits because they mistakenly believed that God's grace was limitless and, therefore, a license to act immorally. Paul reminded his readers that though he was not physically with them, he was present in spirit. This was an expression of intimacy, not a metaphysical presence. As such, Paul had judged the behavior of the man, just as the church should have done when the incident first came to light.

The excommunication suggested by the phrase *hand this man over to Satan* has been difficult for some to grasp. Paul was not suggesting that the man be literally handed over to Satan for his complete destruction. Rather, Paul's hope was that by ceasing contact with the man for a time, the absence of Christ's love through fellowship and the transforming work of the Spirit in spiritual brothers and sisters would lead the man to repent of his wrong doing and come back into fellowship with God and the rest of the body of Christ (salvation in the spirit). Paul consistently used the terms *flesh* and *spirit* to contrast the two ways of orienting one's life. Living in the flesh meant living in opposition to God, while living in the spirit meant living a redeemed life in God through the cross of Christ.

Paul used yeast (leaven) as a metaphor for sin. Just as a small amount of yeast would permeate a whole loaf of bread, so a small amount of sin would permeate a whole life or even a whole body of believers. While the man was guilty of the sin of sexual immorality, the church as a whole was also guilty of sin by failing to deal with the man's sin and holding him accountable.

Paul's earlier letter was not intended to prevent believers from having contact with all immoral people, since it was only through contact that such people would hear about Christ's love, forgiveness and freedom. In this letter Paul instructed his readers to avoid contact with fellow believers who were involved in sexual immorality.

The body of believers was responsible for judging the behavior of their members while judgment of nonbelievers belonged to God.

INSIGHTS

Paul exhorted his readers to rid themselves of all leaven (sin) so as to avoid experiencing sin permeating throughout their lives and church. His exhortation is just as relevant today. Often we think a *white lie* is harmless, or behavior that does not harm anyone else is OK. Such rationales are dangerous. Once a *small* sin is tolerated, it becomes easier to justify something *just a little bit bigger*. The process can continue until one is involved in sin that only a short time ago would have been unthinkable. Better to avoid the temptation altogether by leading a life of integrity and honesty, even if it means starting anew right now.

1. Paul used leaven/yeast as an analogy for how great destruction a small amount of sin can cause. How can we, as Paul suggests, get rid of the old immorality and replace it with the morality of Christ?

2. Paul suggested that we should judge fellow believers' behavior but not that of unbelievers. Why is accountability important?

1 Corinthians, Chapter 6

BACKGROUND

God's Shekinah Glory was the visible representation of His presence in the Old Testament temple (Ex. 40.34). Christ embodied that glory during His life on earth, and it eventually came to reside in all believers through the indwelling of the Holy Spirit (John 14.16-17). The temple did not become obsolete with the coming of Christ but was transformed from a physical building to the body of believers who were (are) indwelt with the Holy Spirit and serve as the visible representation of God on earth.

OVERVIEW

Since believers would one day stand with God in judgment of the rest of the world, Paul contended that disputes between believers should be handled within the church rather than by the courts of the world.

Unlike Roman society in which only the well-to-do served as judges, Paul viewed all believers, even the lowliest, as qualified to judge within the church.

Paul suggested that it was better to be cheated (wronged) by a dishonest person than to witness poorly to the pagan world.

Depending on the context, *the kingdom of God* could refer to either the future time when Christ returns and God's kingdom is established on earth or to the present time as the body of believers spread the good news of Christ throughout the world. As Paul exhorted the Corinthians to live in a manner pleasing to God, he used the term in the former sense.

Paul reminded the Corinthian Christians that those choosing sin over righteousness would not inherit God's kingdom. Paul also encouraged the believers that their faith in Christ had made them righteous before God. He used three verbs to describe what had taken place. The tense of all three indicates an action that had taken place in the past and was complete.

- Washed – spiritually cleansed by God

- Sanctified – holy, set apart

- Justified – declared righteous by God through Christ's work on the cross

All things are lawful (permissible) for me was a popular saying of the time used to justify immoral behavior. Though Christ's death and resurrection had freed believers from the Law of Moses, they were not free to behave in any manner they chose. *Foods for the stomach . . .* was also a saying that was used to justify immoral behavior. The reasoning was that just as one ate food when hungry, so could one indulge in sexual behavior when the craving struck.

Every sin . . . is outside the body was another slogan used to justify sexual immorality. Paul argued that sexual sin was against one's own body. Even worse, however, was that the sin was committed against the Holy Spirit, who resided in the Christian. Such sin desecrated the temple, the believer's body, which was inhabited by God through His Holy Spirit. Since each person was a part of the temple, Paul exhorted each to honor God in the choices made regarding his/her body.

Slaves were *bought at a price* at a slave auction. Paul had this practice in mind when he used the phrase to allude to the redemption available to all people through the blood of Christ. That redemption should lead all to act in such a way that it was evident they belonged to God.

INSIGHTS

Paul's exhortation that the Corinthian Christians not involve themselves in lawsuits against one another is valid even today. Our litigious society encourages us to take our grievances to court, but that should be a last resort and only after at least four previous steps have been taken. Introspection about the situation conducted prayerfully and without anger toward the other party. Second, counsel from an uninvolved and trustworthy Christian. Third, making an effort to find a solution with the other party (Matt. 18.15-17). Fourth, being certain that the lawsuit can be conducted with integrity and without tainting our Christian testimony.[2]

1. How can we and why should we seek the wisdom and counsel of other believers when trying to settle disputes between believers over taking such?

2. Why would Paul suggest it is better to endure being wronged by a dishonest person than it is to give a poor testimony or witness to unbelievers?

[2] *NIV Quest Study Bible* (Grand Rapids, MI: Zondervan, 2003), 1637.

1 Corinthians, Chapter 7

BACKGROUND

Two prevalent views in Paul's time separated the physical and the spiritual. The hedonistic view claimed that sin had only affected the physical body. Believers could sin in their body and not affect their spiritual lives. (Paul addressed this in the previous chapter.) The other believed that anything physical was bad and anything spiritual was good. For this group, to be truly spiritual, all physical desires had to be suppressed. As a result, they endorsed celibacy as the only proper way to live. (Paul addressed that issue here.)

OVERVIEW

After addressing the issues reported to Paul by the members of Chloe's household (1.11), Paul moved to the questions he had received.

The Greek word used to state what is good for a man not to do is better translated *touch* than *marry* (as in the NIV). Many believe *touch* was a euphemism meaning sexual relations.

Paul believed it was better to have a committed relationship with one's spouse than to fulfill sexual temptations through illicit relationships. Each husband and wife was obligated to maintain sexual relations with the other so that neither would be tempted to have sex outside of their marriage.

Paul reiterated Jesus' teaching on the subject of divorce (Mark 10.9-12), though the word he used is translated as depart or separate. In either case, both Paul and Jesus said the same: once married, husbands or wives were not to leave their spouses. Paul addressed an issue Jesus had not: what happened when one spouse became a Christian while the other did not. In that case, Paul encouraged the two to remain together if the unbelieving spouse was willing. Both the unbelieving spouse and any children would be exposed to the teaching of Jesus, which they might not otherwise receive.

Paul next addressed the issue of walking with Christ in whatever manner one was called. Slave or free, each believer was spiritually equal and a slave to Christ. No one was to try to be something s/he was not called to by God.

Paul again stated his opinion that it is better not to marry if one is able. However, choosing to marry is not a sin.

This present distress referred to the time of suffering that was to be experienced by Christians. Paul foresaw a time when marriage would be an encumbrance. Concern for spouse and children could make it difficult and more complicated to live out one's Christian convictions to the fullest.

As the trials came, all things (possessions, mourning, rejoicing, relationships, etc.) were to be held loosely.

The meaning of Paul's exhortation about *any man* and a virgin *past the flower of her youth* is debated. Several interpretations are possible. Paul was perhaps suggesting that if an unmarried man and woman are able to work together for the Lord without their sexual passions being a temptation, they should continue in such manner. But if they could not resist their passions, they should marry.

Marriage was to be a lifelong commitment. Should a marriage partner die, the surviving spouse was free to remarry, though restricted to marrying a fellow Christian. Paul again believed it was better to remain unmarried.

INSIGHTS

Today, many mistakenly believe sex is solely for personal pleasure. God's intention is that sex be a part of a committed, lifelong marriage. It causes spouses to become one flesh, serves to continue the human race, and gives our spirits and souls a taste on earth of the intimacy we will have in heaven with Christ as our bridegroom. While many believe no one is hurt through illicit sexual relationships, the truth is that God's intention overrides human belief. We are all part of the body of Christ and our sin hurts the entire body. Such relations lead to an unintentional bonding that creates great woundedness; wounding that is sometimes evident only years later.

1. For those who are married, what does it mean to live fully as though their bodies were not their own but belonged to their spouse?

2. Paul encouraged spouses to stay married and not leave or divorce one another. In our culture of no-fault divorce, how can we work to ensure our marriages remain strong and committed? How can we encourage other married couples to work through their differences and remain committed to each other?

3. Paul held a commitment to remaining single in high esteem because the single person could focus with great single-mindedness on the work of the Lord. In a culture that puts great value on couples and children, how can we encourage and support those around us who God may call to do His work as a single person?

1 Corinthians, Chapter 8

BACKGROUND

When meat sacrifices were made to pagan gods, a portion of the meat was reserved for the god and the remainder was to be used by the priests. What the priests did not need could be sold at the marketplace. Such meat was freely used by pagans and was often difficult for Christians to avoid, particularly those who had converted from paganism and still had business dealings with pagans or unbelieving family members. Some believed Christians should avoid such tainted meat at all costs while others believed it was acceptable to eat.

OVERVIEW

We know that we all have knowledge is thought to have been a slogan used to justify eating meat offered to idols. While some Christians believed eating such meat was a sin, others believed that since the idols were not real, eating meat offered to them was not a problem. Paul used the term *weak* for those who thought the practice was sinful and *strong* (knowledgeable) for those who thought it was acceptable.

Being in good relationship with God leads to acting in love towards others. Flaunting knowledge over love indicates a lack of real understanding about who God is.

Paul agreed that idols were not real and that there was only one God. He didn't completely dismiss the existence of other gods because they were real in the minds of those who believed in them, even if they weren't physically real.

Paul again equated Jesus Christ with God the Father, stating that all things came to be through them and it is through them that Christians live.

For all but the well-to-do, meat was a luxury that was generally not available except at pagan festivals when it was given to the masses. As a result many Christians associated meat with pagan worship.

Paul consented that the knowledgeable were correct in their views, but he countered that those whose consciences led them to believe eating such meat was sinful might be tempted to eat it and sin if they saw their knowledgeable brothers and sisters eating it. Paul, therefore, exhorted the stronger believers to show love toward the weaker believers by refraining from eating meat sacrificed to idols so their example would not cause their weaker brothers and sisters to stumble.

INSIGHTS

Paul's exhortation to the knowledgeable believers suggests that an act might be OK for one person and sinful for another. Since God speaks individually to His people, He may forbid one from engaging in an activity while allowing another to do so. The key in this situation is to avoid causing a fellow believer to go against what God has directed when and if you engage in the activity that is permissible for you. Paul says that love should be our motivation rather than the personal benefit we get out of the activity. When we truly love those around us, we will want to see them grow in their relationship with Christ, not be hampered by our activities.

1. In Paul's day, idol worship was much more prominent and apparent. While not as obvious today, it is still prevalent. How can we recognize people, things or ideas that have taken the place of God and become idols in our lives? How can we guard against allowing anything taking God's place?

2. Paul cautioned his readers to be aware of doing things that might be stumbling blocks to others. How can things like drinking alcohol or watching certain television programs/movies prove to be stumbling blocks to those around us? How can we be sensitive to inadvertently tempting others with things or activities that are harmless for us?

1 Corinthians, Chapter 9

BACKGROUND

Ancient philosophers and teachers supported themselves in several ways. The most attractive was to become associated with a patron who employed the lecturer to teach at dinners and other similar gatherings. Another method was charging fees for instruction, while yet another was begging (though this method was generally despised). The least attractive means was manual labor. This included the artisan work that Paul would have performed.

OVERVIEW

Paul claimed apostleship based on two assertions. First, he had seen Jesus Christ and second, the body of believers in Corinth was the result of his work in the Lord and served as a seal of his apostleship.

Paul had a right to eat, drink, marry and receive a wage for his work. He chose not to, however, that he might focus exclusively on sharing the gospel of Christ. While the apostles appear to have been married, Paul presented himself and Barnabas as the exception.

Paul quoted Deut. 25.4 to illustrate that even animals are entitled to the fruit for their labor.

Just as the one who sowed seed had a right to enjoy the benefits resulting from the harvest, so Paul should be entitled to the benefits that resulted from his efforts to sow the seed of the gospel among the Corinthians. Moreover, Paul pointed to the priests and Levites who were not only involved in offering sacrifices but were entitled to a portion of some of the sacrifices for their livelihood. Paul, however, did not want to take advantage of that right, lest his motivation for preaching the gospel be seen as what he could get out of such efforts. Paul did not want anything to hinder the effects of the gospel in the lives of those who heard it.

Paul's comment that the *Lord has commanded that those who preach the gospel should live from the gospel* was likely an allusion to Jesus sending the disciples out without food, extra clothing or sandals and relying on those they ministered to for their needs (Luke 10.4-7).

Paul did not preach the gospel because of what he could gain from doing so or even because he chose to, but because God had commanded him to do so.

Paul's highest priority was sharing the gospel with those who needed to hear it. As a result, he gave up his freedom and became a servant and did whatever he could to ensure the gospel message was spread. Though he followed the Law of Moses when he was with Jews but didn't observe it when he was with Gentiles, Paul was clear that he was always under the law of Christ.

Paul used the analogy both of running a race and boxing to convey the need for discipline, sacrifice, consistent practice, and perseverance in order to live the Christian life well.

Some have suggested that being *disqualified* meant losing one's salvation. However, there is a difference between a gift (salvation freely given by God) and a prize (the reward for all effort made for the cause of Christ). Paul was more likely referring to the reward or prize he would receive for the work he did to advance the gospel.

Corinth hosted games every two years that were second in attendance only to the Olympic Games (held every four years). Paul's athletic analogy would have been very familiar to his audience.

INSIGHTS

Paul's desire to live a disciplined, sacrificial, perseverant life in order to ensure the advancement of the gospel is a good example for us today. The world values a life full of comfort and ease. Jesus, however, never promised that following Him would be comfortable or easy. Instead he warned of trials and persecution that would be difficult to endure. We do well to prepare for the difficulties all believers face by being disciplined in our study of God's Word, sacrificial in our accumulation of material goods, and cautious in our consumption of worldly pleasures. Any moments of ease God may grant us should be greatly appreciated.

1. By engaging in manual labor, Paul was using the least attractive means of supporting himself in order to share the gospel with the unbelieving world. In what ways can we check our egos and do what needs to be done in order to be effective witnesses for Christ?

2. Paul used the analogy of running a race to make his point. What analogies and examples can you use to help disseminate in an effective manner the good news of the gospel?

1 CORINTHIANS, CHAPTER 10

BACKGROUND

It was the regular practice in Jewish households for the head of the house to speak a word of thanks or blessing over a cup of wine. Eventually, the last cup of wine at the end of the meal came to be referred to as the *cup of blessing*.

Judaism and many pagan belief systems included sacrifices made at an altar. Anyone who participated in those sacrifices also participated, whether intentionally or not, in the ideology expressed through those sacrifices.

OVERVIEW

Under the cloud, passed through the sea, and *baptized into Moses* all referred to events that took place when the Israelites fled Egypt (Ex. 13-14). The cloud was God's presence, which offered protection and guidance through the desert. The sea was separated to allow the people to cross on dry land. These two experiences *baptized* or brought together all the people under the spiritual leadership of Moses.

The spiritual rock that accompanied them referred to the two instances when God provided water to the Israelites from rocks (Ex. 17.1-5; Num. 20.2-13). In later times, the rock was interpreted as a symbol of the law that could both accompany and sustain them. As Paul looked back on the incidents, however, he substituted Christ for the law and in so doing saw Christ working in the lives of the early Israelites.

Paul pointed to the early Israelites falling into sin due to their inability to resist temptation.

... *rose up to play* (Ex. 32.6) referred to pagan festivities the Israelites engaged in when Aaron made the calf as a substitute for God.

Paul emphasized that what happened to the early Israelites was not confined to history. God's judgment could come to pass on the Corinthians just as easily as it had come on the sins of the Israelites.

Paul's word of hope came from God's mercy; though everyone is tempted, no one would be tempted beyond his or her ability to resist. In addition, God Himself would provide a way to avoid the temptation.

Paul pointed to the unity the believers had as they shared in the body and blood of Christ. At the same time, he warned that pagan worship was a breach of that unity. While the idols themselves had no power, behind the idols were demons that did have power.

Paul had great freedom as he was no longer under the law, but he also had great responsibility. Freedom did not mean entitlement to anything one desired. It had to be exercised within appropriate limits. In so stating, Paul was making a distinction between what the Corinthians had a right to do and what they were obligated to do. Obligations to others are a higher priority than exercising individual rights. As a result, Paul contended that ignorance about whether meat had been offered to idols made it acceptable to eat. If one became aware that it had been offered, it should then be avoided.

Glorifying God should be the ultimate goal of all that is done. Habits and actions may need to be adjusted from time to time depending on the spiritual strength of those in whose company one is. God is glorified when Christ's example is followed.

INSIGHTS

The Devil made me do it! has been a somewhat humorous attempt to avoid taking responsibility for one's own actions. Paul's reminder to the Corinthians can be an encouragement to us today. Temptation *is* common to all people, but God (still) does not allow us to be tempted beyond what we can resist. He gives us a way out every time. The question becomes, "Are we willing to trust that God's ways truly are better than the world's?" If we can say yes, we are well on our way to avoiding the temptations we face. If we answer no, we are more likely to succumb because we do not rely on the strength God makes available to us.

1. What encouragement can we gain from realizing and fully believing that we do not face any temptation that Jesus, himself, has not already faced? How can we use the knowledge that God always provides a way out of temptation to our advantage in dealing with Satan's seductions and enticements?

2. Paul repeatedly quoted Old Testament scriptures and events. How can knowledge of the Old Testament increase and enrich our understanding of New Testament scriptures and the faith we have today?

1 Corinthians, Chapter 11

BACKGROUND

Women's hair was thought to provoke lust in men. As a result, women were expected to cover their hair. Many upper-class women, however, preferred to show off their fashionable hairstyles and did not wear a head covering.

Early believers met in private homes rather than church buildings. Their celebration of the Lord's Supper was preceded by a fellowship meal that became known as the Agape Feast. So many problems arose from such feasts that the Council of Carthage later banned them in 397 A.D.

OVERVIEW

Paul digressed from the issue of food in verse 2-17 to cover the issue of women's head coverings, before returning to questions concerning food once again.

In Paul's time, traditions (teachings) were regulations that were passed on orally. God had not commanded women to cover their heads, but it was a tradition.

Man being the head of woman didn't imply women were inferior to men. Paul stated God was the head of Jesus but did not imply Jesus was inferior to God. Women were equal to men, just as Jesus was equal to God. Each had a different role in God's plan.

In both examples of men and women dishonoring their heads by not covering them, it is unclear whether Paul was referring to their physical or spiritual head. Both interpretations work and both have merit.

Woman from man and *woman for man* both refer to the creation story when God made woman from the man's rib in order to be a helpmate to the man (Gen. 2.20-21). This again, was not a reference to woman's inferiority but to the strength she provided man.

Neither men nor women are independent of the other. Both are created by God to be dependent on one another and on Him.

Paul's reference to nature pointed to how things naturally were. Men and women were naturally different. Each should do what was appropriate to the nature in which they had been created.

Paul changed tacks as he addressed the division that was evident when the Corinthians celebrated the Lord's Supper. Paul could and did praise them for other things, but the divisions that had developed were not praiseworthy.

In Corinth, when well-do-to members opened their homes for church meetings they often seated their social peers in one room and all others in an adjoining room. The social peers enjoyed the best of foods, while the others were served inferior food, creating division and discontent. Paul challenged the believers on such practices and contended that they were not really celebrating the Lord's Supper but merely involved in gluttony and selfishness.

Proclaim the Lord's death until He comes again looked both back in remembrance and forward with hope.

The Lord's Supper was celebrated in *an unworthy manner* when it was eaten with disregard for other members of the church body and Christ's sacrifice. The meal was intended to unite the body and included a time of reflection on what Jesus had done rather than serve as an opportunity to overeat and get drunk. Celebrating in an unworthy manner was evident in the number of people who were weak, sick and asleep (died prematurely, perhaps as a punishment).

INSIGHTS

Today, head coverings for Christian women are not commonplace. Yet the concept presented by Paul is still valid: it is not Christ-like to do that which causes temptation for another. Dressing provocatively, acting seductively, or speaking vulgarly can be temptations to others. We do best to be aware of our surroundings and modify our behavior when it may wrongly influence another. While some would argue they are not responsible for the behavior of those around them, Paul made it clear here and elsewhere that we do not serve Christ well when we intentionally act in ways that do not reflect God's love for His people.

1. Today it is appropriate for a woman to pray with her head uncovered. What other customs or traditions should we honor as a show of respect for God and the church in which we worship?

2. In our culture, we are not encouraged to examine ourselves and confess our wrongdoing. Following this practice and partaking in the body and blood of Christ can lead to participating in communion in a way that dishonors God. Do you regularly spend time examining your life? Are you willing to quickly own your wrongdoing, confess it to others, as necessary, and God?

1 CORINTHIANS, CHAPTER 12

BACKGROUND

Paul's writings contain three references to the types of spiritual gifts (Rom. 12.3-8; 1 Cor. 12.7-11; Eph. 4.11). Each list is different, suggesting that Paul was not giving an exhaustive list. Rather, he was referring to some of the gifts to make his particular point in each letter.

In chapters 12-14, Paul covers the issue of spiritual gifts and how the church should operate in unity while appreciating the diversity of gifts exercised by believers.

OVERVIEW

The Spirit, Lord/Christ and Father all play a role in the distribution of a very diverse set of gifts. The Spirit determines who receives which gift (v. 11). Christ directs the believer in the specific way in which the gift is used within the body (v. 12-24a). The Father created all gifts with equal importance and has coordinated the proper use of the gifts to achieve His plan (v. 24b-26). The diversity of the Trinity is not limited to the Godhead but manifests itself in the body of believers and the gifts they receive.

Paul's list of gifts was likely quite understandable to the Corinthians. Two thousand years later, it is difficult for scholars to agree completely on the meaning of each gift. Likely explanations for each include:

- Word of wisdom – the ability to apply knowledge to address specific needs.

- Word of knowledge – the ability to uncover, collect, study and explain information.

- Faith – the ability to have complete confidence and trust in God for extraordinary deeds.

- Healings – the ability to serve as an intermediary for God's curative and restorative powers.

- Miracles – the ability to serve as a conduit for God's powers that alter the normal course of nature.

- Prophecy – the ability to receive and communicate a direct revelation from God.

- Discerning of spirits – the ability to discern between heavenly and demonic activity.

- Tongues – the ability to speak to God or deliver messages from God in a language never learned.

- Interpretation of tongues – the ability to translate for all to hear the message delivered in tongues[3].

Paul used the human body as an analogy for how the body of Christ should function. The diverse members of the body of Christ were to use their unique gifts for the benefit of all the members, just as the different parts of the human body work together to enable the whole body to function. If one part of the body was hurting, other members were to use their gifts to minister and assist in healing.

Some scholars concede that *earnestly desire* can be translated in the imperative (you should) or the indicative (you do). The indicative fits with the context of chapters 12-14, though it has generally been translated in the imperative. It has been suggested that Paul was exhorting the Corinthians not to seek after the more sensational gifts but to seek instead the *more (most) excellent* gift of love, as he outlines in the next chapter.

---

[3] C. Peter Wagner, *Your Spiritual Gifts* (Ventura, CA: Regal Books, 1979), 102, 158, 218-242

INSIGHTS

Just as in Paul's time, all believers today receive at least one spiritual gift when they come to faith in Christ. That gift(s) is given for the edification and ministry of the body as a whole, not for the individual's personal benefit. Though using our gifts does have personal benefits, it is not the primary purpose. God did not randomly give us spiritual gifts but hand picked each one for us so that we might play a vital role in His plan. Seeking to discover your gift if you don't already know it or using it in the manner God is calling you will lead to a life of adventure, fulfillment and great joy.

1. We can become jealous of other people's God given gifts and the ministry they are called to, forgetting that God has uniquely gifted us to do equally important ministry on His behalf. How can we avoid becoming jealous, rejoice in the ministry of others and utilize our own gifts in a manner that honors God?

2. Paul used the analogy of the body with its many differing parts as a picture of believers. How does this analogy help to explain how a group of believers in a local church as well as the various denominations should strive to work together and appreciate the work and gifts of others?

1 CORINTHIANS, CHAPTER 13

BACKGROUND

God's time of perfection (completion) has been interpreted in a variety of ways. Some believe it was realized at the end of the apostolic era when the core doctrines of the church were established. Others believe it is represented by the completion of the Scriptures that provide the inspired and authoritative source for Christian doctrine. Still others believe this time will occur when Christ returns and believers are transformed.

First Corinthians 13 is the great love chapter of the Bible and is often read at weddings, though its application reaches far beyond romantic love and serves as a framework for extending God's love to all mankind.

OVERVIEW

Whether angels have their own language or not is unknown. Paul's point was even the ability to speak heavenly languages amounts to little without love.

Sounding brass (gong in some translations) and cymbals were instruments used regularly in pagan worship.

Moving mountains was a figure of speech meaning to do the impossible. The implication is ability on its own, regardless of how impossible or unbelievable, is worthless if not done with a spirit of love.

Paul listed some of the characteristics of love:

- patient (suffers long) – willingness to wait when people are not as you would like

- kind – treat people well, regardless of how they treat others
- does not envy – does not show discontentment or resentful feelings toward another
- does not boast/is not proud – doesn't display excessive pleasure in one's abilities, possession or achievements
- is not rude – does not act unfairly or in an inappropriate manner
- is not self seeking – is not selfish; does not put one's own needs ahead of other's needs
- is not provoked (easily angered) – is not overly sensitive or easily irritated
- thinks no evil (keep record of wrongs) – approaches with trust instead of suspicion; keeps no tallies
- does not delight in evil and rejoices in truth – mourns downfalls and celebrates victories
- always protects – prevents harm from being done
- always trusts – shows faith or confidence in a person
- always hopes – endures hardship and rejection while looking forward to a better future
- always perseveres – continues even in the face of difficulty

Through prophesy and other means of God's revelation (His Word, etc.), part of His plan has been revealed, but no believer knows fully all that is to come. When God's time of perfection (or completion) has come, all that is *in part* will fall away.

Paul used *child* five times to show the progression of growth from childhood to adulthood. It served as an illustration of the growth from partial knowledge to the completion that would be realized in God's time through faith in Christ.

Paul used a sequence of *now . . . but then* statements to further make his point that what his readers were currently experiencing was different from what they would experience in the completion of time.

In Paul's time, mirrors were often made of bronze. Even the best mirrors were only able to reflect an image dimly and imperfectly.

Just as love would endure after the grace-gifts were no longer needed, so would faith and hope. Yet even among these three, love is still the most significant.

INSIGHTS

Love is extended by choice, not because of emotion. All too often in our culture we are told to act on our feelings—enjoy love while we feel it, but once it is gone, move on to someone or something else. The love that Paul wrote about and which both God the Father and Jesus modeled throughout the scriptures was not based on emotion. Rather it was a choice to take interest in and look out for another's best interest. It stands on truth and perseveres in difficulty rather than gives up and moves on. Love is so critical to humans because it is often the one thing that can be counted on when everything else seems to be falling apart.

1. Paul writes about the importance of love in the Christian life. In what areas of your life should love play a greater role? Are there people to whom you habitually respond to with something other than love? How can you change your response to them? Who in your life would benefit from the love of God the Father being extended to him through you?

2. Paul presented a long list of love's attributes. Which attributes are strong in your life? Which are weak? How can you implement one, two or more of these attributes to better love the people you meet?

1 Corinthians, Chapter 14

BACKGROUND

Jesus repeatedly treated women with compassion and favor rather than the second-class citizens they were viewed as in His day. By defending their actions (Matt. 26.8-13) and approaching them when others wouldn't (John 4.5-42), He established a new standard in which women should be treated. Paul continued in that vein by suggesting women ask questions of their husbands at home. Since women were not afforded the education men received, he was encouraging them to learn and grow in knowledge. In effect, Paul was encouraging men to ensure women received an education.

OVERVIEW

Verse 1 serves as a pivot to connect what preceded with what follows.

The Greek word for desire can mean to *run after*, *aspire*, or *hasten*. Many things in life can be optional, but Paul stated that love should be earnestly sought after.

The same note regarding *earnestly desiring* applies here that applied to its use in chapter 12. Paul may have been stating, *seek out spiritual gifts* (as many translators have rendered). Alternatively, he may have meant, *you are wanting other gifts when you should be wanting prophecy*.

Paul's use of prophecy in this section may refer to all the speaking gifts (v. 6). Whether all the speaking gifts or prophecy itself, it was contrasted to the gift of tongues. One could be easily understood while the other was either communication between the speaker and God or needed an interpreter to be understood.

Paul encouraged spontaneity in prayers, even praying in tongues. He instructed those who prayed in tongues to also pray for someone who could interpret, so that the body as a whole would benefit from the prayer.

Paul may have picked up on his analogy in 13.11 as he instructed the Corinthians to be mature in understanding but to be infants when it came to malice (evil).

As Paul continued his instruction on the use of tongues, he was more concerned with how its use by the whole body would affect unbelievers, who were much more likely to respond positively to what they understood (prophesy) than what they could not comprehend (tongues).

Spiritual gifts were for the edification of the body of believers. Though many members may have been able to contribute, Paul urged his readers to exercise constraint and maintain orderly activities, allowing members with varying gifts the opportunity to edify the whole.

Exercising a spiritual gift was not license to speak without restraint. What was spoken was open for judgment by the church to ensure it did not stray from God's Word.

There is no mention of women keeping silent in any of the laws handed down from God to any of His prophets. Since women in Paul's time were generally uneducated they may have had questions about teachings that men already understood. Paul had previously recognized women prophesying (only speaking against their head coverings, 11.5), so it is unlikely that he was later condemning a practice he initially appeared to approve. Paul's comments concerning women appear in the midst of other comments that encourage his readers to maintain order during their gatherings. Though the role of women in the church has been and continues to be debated, it is unlikely Paul believed they were only to observe the proceedings and not be involved in ministry.

INSIGHTS

Paul's belief that spiritual gifts were for the benefit of the church as a whole is worth noting. It can be tempting to exercise God-given gifts with the wrong motivation. We may feel prideful about what we can do, compare our ability to others' inability, seek out the acclaim that accompanies our giftedness or be completely focused on advancing our careers. None of these motivations minister with the heart of Jesus, who was completely focused on the recipient of His ministering. Jesus cared much less about His own personal well-being and much more about the soul and salvation of those to whom He ministered.

1. Paul encouraged his readers to eagerly desire spiritual gifts. What is/ are your spiritual gift(s)? How is God calling you to use your gifting to build His Kingdom and spread the good news of Jesus Christ?

2. Paul spoke at great length about the gift of tongues. Today, people have often manipulated what appears to be the gift of tongues to fit their own agenda. How can you ensure that gift of tongues, if God has given you this true gift, or any other spiritual gift you are blessed with, is used in ways that honor God and are in accordance with His will?

1 Corinthians, Chapter 15

BACKGROUND

The Old Testament sacrificial system, which God handed down to Moses, included the Feast of Weeks when a portion of the harvested crops and newborn livestock were offered as a sacrifice to God. These offerings were called firstfruits and recognized the blessing God had given through the harvest. God also claimed the first-born son be dedicated to Him (Ex. 22.29). The tribe of Levi was later dedicated to serving and maintaining the Temple and served as a substitute for the first-born sons.

OVERVIEW

Though the Corinthians disputed some things about their faith, Paul argued that they could not dispute the physical resurrection of Jesus. Paul contended the resurrection was an established fact and he preached the good news to the Corinthians based on this fact.

As Paul spoke about Christ's resurrection, he used the perfect tense of the Greek word for *rose*. Used in such a manner, Paul stressed the continuing impact of the resurrection.

Paul's mention of the witnesses still living was an invitation to his readers to check out for themselves the truthfulness of what he stated.

Paul emphasized his own unworthiness to be called an apostle because of his history in persecuting the very church he was later called to serve. It was only because of God's grace and forgiveness that he was able to minister rather than stand condemned.

Paul laid out a well-conceived argument to counter the teaching of some Corinthians that believers would not rise from the dead. Paul stated that the crux of Christian beliefs was predicated on Jesus' resurrection. Without that belief, the faith of the Corinthians (and all Christians) amounted to nothing.

Just as death came through the sin of Adam, so life came through the perfect sacrifice of Jesus, who served as the firstfruits offering on behalf of all humanity. Jesus not only serves as the deliverer for humanity but also as the conqueror of all that is evil and will deliver the kingdom to God, at which time the kingdom of God will be established on earth.

Jesus will one day reign over all things with one exception – God the Father, to whom Jesus will be subject.

The meaning of *baptism of the dead* has been debated for centuries. The most likely explanation is that the Corinthians had adopted a pagan practice of being baptized on behalf of those who had already died or those who had come to faith but died before they could be baptized. Whatever the explanation, Paul did not debate the practice. Instead, he pointed to the contradiction that existed between engaging in such a practice (which indicated belief in some type of life after death) and denying the reality of the resurrection of the dead.

Paul encouraged his readers not to dismiss the reality of the resurrection just because it was too hard to understand. Paul used the analogy of a seed being sown. It dies to itself in order to produce the plant that comes from it. No plant is sown in order to grow a different kind of plant. Paul also pointed to the variety of animals and celestial bodies as proof that the God who could create such variety could also resurrect a new, incorruptible body from a deceased, corruptible human body.

Paul argued that the hope of the coming resurrection took the power out of death and in so doing out of the condemnation associated with sin.

INSIGHTS

Just as the Corinthians did, we can be tempted to discount that which we do not understand. This can leave us in a quandary because we will never understand God completely. He reveals aspects of Himself, but there is much that remains hidden. If we discount what we don't understand, we risk missing God's work in our lives and in the lives of those around us as we lament the birth of an autistic child, battle a life threatening cancer, endure a devastating divorce or struggle through a job loss. Our lack of understanding does not mean God is incapable. It just provides us with the opportunity to have faith and trust in Him.

1. Until he had a personal encounter with Jesus Christ, Paul persecuted Christians. He went from persecutor of Christianity to defender and one of the most effective evangelists the world has known. As you encounter Jesus, what areas of your life does He want to redeem, to cover with the blanket of His truth? To whom might God be calling you to speak about Jesus as result of your own experience with Him?

2. Paul suggested that his readers needed to stand firm on the gospel. Is there any part of the gospel's good news – we are saved by faith, Christ's death paid the penalty for our sins, His resurrection defeated death and allows us to experience eternal life – that you do not wholeheartedly believe? What do you need to release to God or believe by faith in order to experience the power of the gospel?

1 Corinthians, Chapter 16

BACKGROUND

Timothy and Apollos were Paul's co-workers. Timothy was converted at an early age and later worked for the Lord under Paul's guidance. Apollos taught an incomplete gospel until Aquila and Priscilla enlightened him. Stephanas, Fortunatus, and Achaicus likely traveled from Corinth to Ephesus to report on the problems in their city and bring the questions Paul addressed. Aquila and Priscilla, originally from and likely known by many in Corinth, accompanied Paul to Ephesus where they then settled.

OVERVIEW

The monetary collection Paul was asking for from the Corinthians would be taken to Jerusalem, where there is evidence that a famine had gripped the surrounding area. The collection was likely taken to help believers there.

In the Old Testament, God established the practice of the people giving a tithe to support those who maintained the temple as well as to help those in need. The New Testament does not specify the ten percent mentioned in the Old Testament but does continue the tradition of generously supporting those in need.

The great and effective door referred to ministry opportunities presenting themselves to Paul. He did not want to leave before he had a chance to complete all the Lord was calling him to do.

Paul encouraged the Corinthian believers to do four things: watch (be on guard), stand fast (firm) in the faith, be brave and be strong. *Watch* was often used in the New Testament to point to the expectation of an event that was yet to occur. *Stand fast* was an exhortation motivated by the subject of the letter. The Corinthians had been vulnerable to false teaching. To counter this, they needed to be confident in what Paul had taught them. *Be brave* could also be translated as *play the man* or *act like men* and pointed to maturity as much as bravery. *Be strong* is translated from a Greek word used only four times in the New Testament. Its meaning includes a sense of continuing progress. Becoming strong was not a one-time event but a continuing effort. Paul balanced these four with a reminder that everything the Corinthians did was to be done with love.

O Lord, come is translated from the Aramaic words *marana tha*, which had quickly become a common expression pointing to the return of Christ.

INSIGHTS

Paul included a curse on those who did not believe in Christ in his closing remarks to the Corinthians. This may seem a harsh statement but pointed to the seriousness of choosing or refusing to place one's faith in Christ. Today the choice is just as serious and its ramifications are realized not only during our lifetimes but in the after life as well. Eternal life or eternal death is the consequence of our decision here in the present time. *Eternal* is almost beyond human comprehension. Everlasting. Perpetual. Continual. Never-ending. For those who have not yet made the decision, these words are worth contemplating. Then decide where you want to spend your existence after your earthly life: in heaven with God and those who love you, or in hell, alone, without love and tormented for eternity.

1. Paul reminded the people to be on guard, be faithful, courageous, strong and motivated by love. If Paul were here today, would he see these characteristics in your life? If not, what changes do you need to make so that they are?

2. As your income allows, do you generously support those in need? If God is calling you to give more than you are comfortable giving, are you able to trust that He will meet your needs as you obediently do as God calls?

SECOND CORINTHIANS

Second Corinthians is the most autobiographical of all Paul's writings. His emotions are evident as he writes about the joys, sorrows, aspirations, and disappointments he's experiencing as a result of reports from the church.

Paul's motivation for writing 2 Corinthians was concern for the church. The believers had responded well to his previous letter and Paul had received a good report from Titus. However, he had also heard that false teachers were still influencing the believers. In an attempt to promote their own message, these false teachers were discrediting Paul and attacking his character. In an effort to ensure that the gospel of Christ was not compromised, Paul defended his authority and message. Even as he stated his defense, his writing shows concern and love for the church he planted and the people he wanted to know the fullness of true faith in Christ.

The first two thirds (chapters 1-9) of Paul's letter is joyful and exuberant. The tone changes in the last third (chapters 10-13) to one that is much firmer and more defensive. Some scholars have suggested that these chapters were not part of the original letter.

BACKGROUND

Achaia was a Roman province with Corinth as its major city. It encompassed what is now southern Greece.

Asia was a Roman province whose capital was Ephesus. It covered much of what is now western Turkey.

OVERVIEW

Paul used the standard ancient letter writing introduction by including a salutation, naming the author(s) and the recipients and offering a greeting. Timothy was listed as a coauthor.

Paul used the same Greek word, translated as both comfort and consolation in various texts, ten times in verses 3-7. The meaning included a sense of encouraging others in their faith and as they endured hardships.

Paul experienced a great deal of persecution in Ephesus (Acts 19.23-41) and it is likely that to which he referred.

Paul returned to the theme of death and resurrection several times throughout this letter. He had already faced death when his persecutors attempted to stone him.

Paul related his trials not in an effort to make others feel sorry for him but to show how God had answered the Corinthians' prayers for him. The answered prayers were reason to enthusiastically praise God.

Paul began early to defend himself against opposition shown to him by false teachers in Corinth. He had acted in Godly wisdom, not the fleshly wisdom of selfishness.

Paul had intended to visit Corinth, both on his way to and return from Macedonia. He had been unable to do so, causing his critics to accuse him of living according to the flesh.

Our word referred to Paul's teaching, which he also defended against his critics.

Yes and no referred to something that was contradictory and inconsistent. The Greek phrasing of Paul's questions indicates he expected a negative response.

Just as Christ's message was true, so was the message Paul and his companions had preached.

The evidence of Paul's authority is attested to by the anointing of the Holy Spirit. A seal showed ownership of a document and verified it had not been tampered with. God's seal on Paul claimed Paul as God's own and verified Paul's ministry and teaching.

Paul's motivation for visiting Corinth was to straighten out the problems that had been reported to him. He ultimately changed his plans in order to give the Corinthians an opportunity to address their own issues.

INSIGHTS

Paul stated that the trials he endured would serve as comfort for his readers. The comfort we receive from God during our trials becomes a gift we may well have the opportunity to pass on to others enduring their own trials. We may not understand the reasons for the trial we are called to endure. It may seem senseless in the greater scheme of life, but God does not waste anything. The comfort we experience during a trial can show us the way to comfort others. Unwillingness to share this comfort can point to a lack of sincere faith in God. Willingness to share it can bring unimaginable hope to others.

1. Paul was careful not to boast in his own achievements but only in the grace and wisdom of God. Are there areas in your life where you take credit that belongs to God? How can you better live in simplicity, holiness and sincerity?

2. As believers, we, too, can stand firm in Christ, knowing we are anointed by Him, and have God's seal of ownership, the Holy Spirit, in our hearts. Do you fully and confidently believe this is true? Do you allow and can you appreciate the work God does in you and through you as a result?

2 Corinthians, Chapter 2

BACKGROUND

Triumphal processions were a common part of Roman victory celebrations. After a victorious war, a general would lead his army and captives in a parade along the main street. Priests often followed the conqueror with censers of burning incense.

OVERVIEW

Continuing on his reason for not visiting Corinth as planned, Paul stated he did not want to bring further sorrow to the believers. His sorrow would likely have come in the way of a reprimand or effort to correct that which contradicted his earlier teachings.

Scholars have debated whether Paul's mention of his previous writing refers to 1 Corinthians, or chapters 10-13 of 2 Corinthians, or a letter that has since been lost.

Paul may have been referring to the good outcome that came from disciplining the offender mentioned in his previous letter (1 Cor. 5). However, Paul does not mention the offense, so there is no certainty that this was the case. Whoever the offender, Paul stipulated that discipline was for the purpose of repentance and restoration. Forgiveness needed to follow discipline, so that the offender might be restored into the fellowship of the body of believers. Vindication had no place in discipline, which must be accompanied by love.

Paul's request that the church extend forgiveness was a test of their obedience to Christ. Would they do as Christ commanded and Paul taught?

The discipline and forgiveness of the church body was sufficient for Paul; he would also extend forgiveness. Forgiveness by the church showed their obedience to Christ and removed the opportunity for Satan to gain a foothold in the church.

Beginning with 2.14, Paul starts a long digression that lasts through 7.4. At that point he again picks up the story of his trip to Macedonia.

Paul used the Roman victory procession as an analogy for the praises due God. God was the conquering general who led Paul and other believers in the victory procession. Like incense in censers, the people disseminated the sweet aroma of the knowledge of Christ.

The fragrance of Christ was realized not by the number of converts or respondents to the message but through obedience to preaching the gospel.

Both life and death were represented in the Roman procession through the victorious soldiers and the captives destined for judgment or slavery. Likewise, both were represented in the procession Paul envisioned. Those who accepted the gospel message were destined for life while those who rejected it would see death.

Some were prone to adapt (peddle) the gospel message for their own personal gain. For Paul, however, the gospel message was sufficient. He was sincere in his preaching and he looked for no personal gain from it.

INSIGHTS

In the *me-first* attitude of today's culture, Paul's desire to preach the gospel at no personal gain and often while suffering personal loss can seem quite foreign. This attitude was not Paul's alone. It was motivated by what Jesus had already done on the cross. Had Jesus had the same *me-first* attitude, He never would have suffered the terrible death on a cross, much less left heaven. His willingness to set his own comfort and rights aside allows us to reconcile our relationship with God the Father. Likewise, our willingness to set aside our comfort and rights can lead someone else into a reconciled relationship with God.

1. Do you extend forgiveness as easily and quickly as God extends it to you? Are you willing to extend forgiveness out of obedience to God even when it is hard to do so?

2. What does it mean to be the fragrance or aroma of Christ among those being saved and those perishing?

2 Corinthians, Chapter 3

BACKGROUND

It was common for Jewish travelers to carry with them letters of recommendation. These letters could be written by anyone who was trustworthy and served to inform a host of the reliability and honesty of the traveler. In addition to affirming the trustworthiness of a traveler to receive food and lodging, such letters could also serve as an introduction for the traveler in a distant city.

Moses' encounter with God affected him so deeply his face shone, causing the people to draw back in fear (Ex. 34.29-30).

OVERVIEW

Though the Corinthians had come to know Paul during his stay with them, he wondered if he needed to obtain a letter of recommendation in order to reassure them of his trustworthiness. On the other hand, Paul was certain he did not need a letter of recommendation on behalf of the Corinthians because he already had one. Through his ministry to the Corinthians, God had written their letter of recommendation directly on his heart.

Paul noted that his ministry to the Corinthians was not done through his own strength but by the power of God.

The letter that kills refers to the Law God handed down to Moses. That Law itself did not kill, but the penalty for not following it was death. Since no one could keep it perfectly, all were destined to die. The Law pointed to the need for another means of reconciling with God, which was provided through the new covenant.

Paul pointed out three contrasts between the Old Testament and New Testament ministries. Each contrast begins with the word *if* (vv. 7, 9, 11):

- Though the law *engraved on stones* (Ten Commandments) was glorious, the ministry of the Spirit was even more glorious.

- The law was holy, but it pointed to condemnation and death. The ministry of the Spirit, however, points to life and gives eternal life.

- The old ministry was passing away but the new one would remain.

Moses used a veil to hide the glory on his face, but it also concealed when the glory passed away. In a similar manner, the people had a veil over their hearts that prevented them from seeing the passing away of the old ministry. Just as Moses removed the veil whenever he spoke to God, so the people could remove the veil on their hearts by turning to Christ.

The Spirit is God Himself and is present in the new covenant just as He was present in the old.

Faith in Christ not only means believers have an unveiled face, but also that they are continually being transformed to more and more reflect the glory of God through the power of the Spirit. (This process is called sanctification.)

INSIGHTS

Paul found his sufficiency and confidence not in his own ability but in the power and strength he found in God. Just as Paul could have preached the gospel through his own power, we are often tempted to do the work God has given us through our own strength. Sometimes we fail to realize and other times forget, that we have very little power on our own (though the world would have us believe otherwise). It is only by relying on God to provide what is needed at the time it is needed that we are able to accomplish anything of lasting value. God is able to work through us in ways we can't begin to imagine when we rely on Him.

1. Paul says we are not sufficient ourselves, but that our sufficiency comes from God. What does this mean? How and why has God made us sufficient ministers of His new covenant?

2. Why does Paul refer to the Law Moses received as the ministry of death? How is the ministry of the Spirit more glorious than the ministry of the law?

2 Corinthians, Chapter 4

BACKGROUND

Slaves of high-ranking officials often had more power and control of more wealth than the average person. Though these slaves lacked the personal freedom of the average person, they wielded great authority.

Clay was readily available in the ancient Near East and was used extensively for making pots and other containers. Because clay was so readily available, pots made from it were cheaper and more disposable than containers made from other materials such as bronze.

OVERVIEW

Lose heart means to become discouraged or grow weary. Paul had confidence that he had received the gospel message from God and was called to preach it. That confidence prevented him from becoming discouraged.

Because Paul ministered according to the call of God and through the strength God had given him, he denied any charges that he had in any way altered the message of God.

Continuing the veil theme, Paul pointed to the *god of this world* or Satan as the one who prevented unbelievers from hearing and comprehending the gospel message.

Paul uses the phrase *bondservant* or *slave* of Christ as a title of honor. He recognized his role as servant to Christ but also understood Christ had entrusted him with great responsibility.

Paul referred to the divine revelation of Christ as a treasure and the human body as a clay pot (earthen vessel). God allowed His great treasure to be set inside a common, everyday, fragile pot! By doing so, God caused the focus to be on His glory, not on the vessel that proclaimed it.

Paul's later use of *every side* infers outside and inside (7.5), therefore he may have been referring to all the emotions he was experiencing as well as what was going on around him.

Despite all the forces opposing Paul, nothing could bring him to utter hopelessness. He linked his suffering to the death of Christ, which he then carried within himself. By so doing the power of the living Christ was displayed through Paul's life.

Paul's willingness to experience death allowed the Corinthians to experience eternal life.

Paul quoted Psalm 116.10 to show his willingness to suffer persecution in order to speak the gospel. He was able to take comfort in what he knew to be true about God rather than what he may have felt at any given moment.

The outward man referred to the physical body while the inward man referred to the spirit. One would perish while the other would have an eternal existence. One was deteriorating and dying while the other was being renewed and revitalized.

Paul's focus on eternal life and all its glory allowed him to put the momentary affliction he suffered into perspective. That change in perspective also led him to look to what was unseen, knowing that those things were what had the most value and significance.

INSIGHTS

Paul stated that just as Jesus' death was a precursor to his resurrection and eternal life, so the suffering Paul endured was a precursor to the eternal life experienced by those who believed the gospel message he preached. The same is true for us today. God does not allow believers' suffering to go to waste (Rom. 8.28). As we trust in God and lean into Him when things get difficult, He will use our suffering to bring glory to Himself and unbelievers to faith in His Son. As a result, those things that are most difficult to endure have the potential to bring us great hope.

1. How can you join Paul in not losing heart as we minister to others? How can we ensure we present the Truth without deceitfully manipulating God's Word in any way?

2. How have you experienced being hard-pressed, perplexed, persecuted, struck down, yet not crushed, in despair, forsaken or destroyed? How does experiencing these things allow us to identify with Christ's death and resurrection? How are we made more and more into the image of Christ because of these experiences?

2 Corinthians, Chapter 5

BACKGROUND

Rome had two kinds of provinces, senatorial and imperial. Senatorial provinces were those that had submitted to Roman rule, were under the control of the Senate and were generally on good terms with Rome. Imperial provinces had been acquired later, were under the authority of the emperor, and often were not as peaceful as the senatorial provinces. To help ensure good relations and peace with Rome, the emperor appointed ambassadors to serve in the imperial provinces.

OVERVIEW

Building on the final three verses of the previous chapter, Paul compared the human body to a tent. Just as a tent was a temporary dwelling and would not endure forever, so the human body would one day die and decompose. Each believer has a permanent house, prepared by God, waiting and ready for occupancy.

As believers endure suffering, they long for the better life they know they will experience once they receive their resurrected bodies. That longing does not mean they wish to cut this life short, but that the splendor of what is to come is so much better than the current suffering being endured.

God Himself has prepared each believer for what is to come and has sent His Spirit as a promise or assurance of that future.

Though believers do not yet completely experience life with God, the Holy Spirit's guarantee gives each confidence for the present.

Since Jesus cannot be seen, believers must live by their faith in Him.

The goal of all believers at all times should be to do what is pleasing to God. This is especially true as one day all will stand before God in judgment of what they have done while on earth.

The terror of the Lord referred to the fear Paul perceived at the thought of standing before God in judgment. That fear motivated him to share the gospel message. In the immediate context, Paul wanted to persuade the Corinthians of his integrity and sincerity and the resulting truthfulness of the gospel message he preached.

Paul's defense of his ministry and the gospel message he preached was motivated by the desire to give the Corinthians both understanding and a defense against the teachers who were preaching a false gospel. Paul's purpose in exposing himself to danger (*beside ourselves, out of our mind*) was to glorify God, just as his soundness (rightness) of mind was an assurance to the Corinthians.

Christ's death on the cross was followed by the death of all believers to their sin, and because believers no longer lived in their sin, they lived for Christ.

God used Christ's death and resurrection to reconcile a fallen world to Himself. That ministry of reconciliation started with Jesus and was passed on to believers that they might further extend reconciliation throughout the world.

Just as the emperor used ambassadors to extend peace in his kingdom, so God sent believers into the world as ambassadors of His message of reconciliation.

Jesus was not made *to be sin* by sinning Himself, but because He carried the burden of all of humanity's sin when He died as the reconciling sacrifice on the cross. This allows believers to stand in righteousness before God.

INSIGHTS

Many people today say that they could never believe in what they cannot see. They use this as a reason to reject the message of Christ. Yet their very life is dependent on faith. Each breath they take is an act of faith. They cannot see the air, yet they continue to breath, having faith that the needed oxygen will be brought into their bodies. Love is another thing that cannot be seen, yet some people will go to great lengths to experience the love they were deprived of as children. The need to walk by faith rather than by sight is no more unrealistic in relation to faith in Christ than it is in relation to the very act of living.

1. What does it mean to walk by faith and not by sight? How do we walk by faith on a daily basis? Why is walking in faith in God so important?

2. Paul told his readers that their faith in Christ made them new creations. How have you experienced this? In your life, what old things have you seen pass away to be replaced by new virtues?

2 Corinthians, Chapter 6

BACKGROUND

In all his epistles, Paul addressed his readers directly on only three occasions (2 Cor. 6.11; Gal. 3.1; Phil 4.15). Each was accompanied by a determined expression of emotion.

In many respects, associations, guilds and societies dominated Corinth. There was an organization for almost every aspect of life and each had its idol. Any disobedience to an idol would supposedly bring the wrath of the god on the whole guild. As a result believers often tried to appease an idol even though they did not believe in it.

OVERVIEW

The Corinthian church would believe in vain if they put their faith in Christ and then failed to live for Him. They would not receive the heavenly reward that was promised for all who worked to advance God's kingdom during their lifetimes.

Paul quoted from Isaiah 49.8 to indicate that God was ready to listen to the Corinthian believers. Though salvation was assured at the time they placed their faith in Christ (justification), it is worked out through Christ's work in us over time (sanctification) until the time believers receive their resurrected bodies (glorification). God would guide anyone through the process if they would simply turn to Him.

Paul and his co-workers conducted themselves in such a way as to be blameless and righteous before God in all they did. Paul listed various experiences in which they found themselves:

- suffering they endured (vv. 4-5);

- behaviors they had chosen (vv. 6-7);

- paradoxical experiences they had (vv. 8-10).

Paul included a highly emotional section (6.11-7.4) beseeching the Corinthians to return to the intimate relationship they had originally had with him. The accusations against Paul as well as the false teaching that had been circulating had caused the Corinthians to emotionally withdraw.

Paul drew from the Old Testament command not to yoke an ox and a donkey together when he urged the Corinthians not to be unequally yoked (Deut. 22.10). A concept often quoted regarding marriage (a believer was not to marry an unbeliever), Paul suggested that believers should not connect themselves to unbelievers in consequential ways.

Belial is used only here in the New Testament and referred to one who was foul and evil.

Paul quoted several scripture references in verses 16-18 in order to make his point (Lev. 26.11; Is. 52.11 with Ezek. 20.34; 2 Sam. 7.14 with Is. 43.6). He was not suggesting that believers avoid contact with unbelievers but that they not engage in any of the sinful practices or hold any of the ungodly values of the unbelievers.

INSIGHTS

Paul's caution to the Corinthian believers about not becoming unequally yoked is worth contemplating today. Many times believers have entered into contracts, business partnerships and other immutable relationships with unbelievers only to find after it's too late that the unbeliever has different values, is unscrupulous or in some other manner compromises the integrity of the believer. Such relationships can be legally binding and very difficult to get out of once the truth becomes known. When contemplating such relationships, great care must be taken, and the wisest course of action may be to avoid the commitment altogether.

1. Paul was intentional about being blameless and righteous before God. Since Paul still experienced moments when he sinned, how could he say he was blameless and righteous? How can you adopt a similar attitude and be blameless and righteous before God?

2. Paul told his readers not to be unequally yoked with unbelievers. Why is this important? Beyond marriage, what areas of life might this instruction apply to? What are some of the pitfalls of spiritually, legally, emotionally or physically connecting ourselves to unbelievers?

2 CORINTHIANS, CHAPTER 7

BACKGROUND

The first two kings of Israel poignantly illustrate Paul's contrast of godly and worldly sorrow. Saul repeatedly defended his decision to disobey the Lord when confronted by Samuel. His insincere confession was given only when he was faced with the consequences of his actions (1 Sam. 15). David, on the other hand, offered immediate and sincere repentance when confronted by Nathan. Though his repentance did not prevent the consequences from occurring, he did retain God's favor and blessing (2 Sam. 12).

OVERVIEW

Building on his statements in the previous chapter, Paul exhorted the Corinthians to cleanse themselves both physically and spiritually; encompassing actions, behaviors, attitudes and thoughts. All were to be purified so as to live in righteousness before a holy God.

Paul earnestly desired a restoration of his relationship with the Corinthians. The damaged relationship had resulted from the allegations leveled by the false teachers who needed to discredit Paul's teaching in order to advance their own. Paul asserted he had done nothing to harm or take advantage of the Corinthians.

Paul had been distressed when he could not find Titus (2.12-13) and was relieved not only to find him but ecstatic that the Corinthians accepted the exhortations contained in his previous letter.

In ancient times, written or spoken rebukes were reserved for only the most severe of transgressions. It was generally believed that recipients would respond better if praise and reproof were mixed together. The distress Paul felt at sending such a letter to the Corinthians was turned into joy when he learned they had received it in good faith.

Sorrow over wrongdoing can be motivated by being caught or suffering the consequences of the sin. Godly sorrow, however, is motivated by a sincere regret for offending God by sinning. Such sorrow leads to repentance, restoration of relationship with God and spiritual deliverance (salvation).

Paul praised the Corinthians for their response to his letter and for their amending their wrongdoings. In ancient rhetoric, repeating related terms emphasized the meaning of those terms.

Paul had boasted about the Corinthians to Titus before sending him to them. His boastings had proven to be accurate and Titus, too, had good memories of his time with them. Such response had given Paul great joy and confidence in the Corinthian believers.

INSIGHTS

Paul wrote his letter of rebuke out of sincere concern for the Corinthians, and then experienced trepidation at the thought of how they would receive it. Many of us experience a similar sequence of emotions when we confront those making sinful choices. Our certainty in following God's call and lead in our lives can be followed by doubt about how the recipients may react. While we are not guaranteed the positive outcome Paul experienced, we can find comfort in our obedience to God. We are not responsible for how others react, yet are responsible for doing what God calls us to do. God will bless our obedience whatever the response from the recipients.

1. Paul commended the Corinthian church for experiencing godly sorrow. How does godly sorrow produce repentance leading to salvation? Why is repentance such an important part of the Christian walk? Is there anything you need to repent of before God?

2. The church at Corinth had to respond to a strong and justified rebuke from Paul. How do you deal with justified rebukes from others? Are you willing to listen and take to heart what is said? How does God use such rebukes to mold you into the likeness of Christ?

2 CORINTHIANS, CHAPTER 8

BACKGROUND

Macedonia encompassed the region that is now northern Greece. Paul had planted several churches within the region, including those in Philippi, Thessalonica and Berea.

Scholars have suggested that one of Titus' companions could have been Luke, Barnabas, Silas, Timothy or John Mark, though there is no way of knowing with certainty.

OVERVIEW

God's grace on the churches in Macedonia enabled them to give generously, joyfully and freely even as they experienced trials, poverty and gave beyond their means. They were so blessed by giving that they urgently pleaded for the opportunity to give to those in need.

The Corinthian believers had an abundance of spiritual gifts. Blessings came both from giving and using one's spiritual gifts. Paul did not want the Corinthians to experience blessing in one area and miss out in the other.

Paul outlined some of the principles that apply to properly motivated giving. It should be:

- motivated by love
- guided by one's willingness and capacity
- and shared equally by the members of the body

Paul's request was not given as a command. Rather generosity was one result of sincere love. Jesus' love for all people motivated Him to give up the riches of heaven for the poverty of earth in order that all on earth may experience heavenly riches. Likewise, believers should be motivated by love to give some of their riches so that those who are poor in spirit (unbelievers) and those in need might also experience greater richness.

Paul encouraged the Corinthians to finish what they had started; doing so would be profitable (to their advantage). Such profit could be realized during their lifetime but would certainly be realized at the judgment seat of Christ.

The equality of giving was not realized strictly in value of what was given but in each person's ability to give; the burden should not fall on only a few but be shared by all. Equality was also realized as one gave out of their abundance and later received in their need. God supplies *enough* to the body of believers, though it is often the responsibility of the believers to ensure it is sufficiently distributed. As proof, Paul pointed to the manna that sustained the Israelites during their forty-year desert experience (Ex. 16.18). '

Paul included a note of recommendation for Titus and his companions. Such a note is similar to the letter of recommendation Paul wondered if the Corinthians needed on his behalf earlier in the letter (3.1).

The comment that Titus went *of his own accord* likely means he paid his own way.

Titus' companions were men of high repute. The first was chosen by the churches to accompany Titus (v.18-19) while the second had distinguished himself in ministry (v. 22-23).

INSIGHTS

Paul gave a strong admonition to the Corinthians to give willingly and generously. This is often in direct opposition to the message of the world. Today we are often inundated with messages about looking out for *number one*, saving for a rainy day, desiring a life of leisure and hanging on to all one can get. Such messages promote selfishness, rather than generosity; personal comfort rather than sacrifice for the good of others; and living in abundance rather than adequacy. Such messages are also at cross purposes with God's desire to meet His people's needs through the abundance of others.

1. Paul told his readers that despite great trials and deep poverty, the Macedonian church experienced great joy because they freely gave beyond their ability in order to bless those in need. Has God called you to give more than you think you can? Can you take a step of faith by responding in obedience? Why do you think God allows such abundant joy to come from helping those in need?

2. Paul encouraged the Corinthian believers to finish what they had started. Has God called you to any work that you have started but not finished, or not started at all? What keeps you from finishing? To whom can you turn for encouragement?

2 Corinthians, Chapter 9

BACKGROUND

In the agrarian cultures of Paul's time, it was well known that what was harvested depended upon what was sown, just as the amount of the harvest was affected by the amount of seed sown. These principles were applied throughout scripture as analogies for other parts of life. Paul applied the principle to giving (9.6), as did the writer of Proverbs (11.24). The principle is also applied to the choices one makes (Job 4.8; Prov. 22.8; Gal. 6.7-10).

OVERVIEW

Ministering (service) to the saints referred to the offering Paul was hoping to collect.

Rivalries often developed between cities or regions and Paul played on a likely rivalry by comparing Achaia (whose capital was Corinth) to Macedonia. He also employed the rhetorical technique of endearment by boasting about the Corinthian church. Such boasting, however, put Paul's honor at risk if the church did not live up to his praises.

The *brethren* Paul sent ahead of time would have been Titus and his companions (8.16-23).

Paul applied the principle of sowing and reaping to giving not as an absolute law but as a general principle. God ultimately determines the outcome of one's giving. In general the giver will reap from the giving; timing and amount are left to God's direction that His plan might be fulfilled.

Paul did not want the body of believers to be forced into giving or to give grudgingly. Rather he wanted them to be settled in their own hearts as to how much was to be given and then do it with a joyful spirit.

Paul quoted from Psalm 112.9, likely using the verse to indicate that those who give to the poor will be rewarded with everlasting righteousness.

Paul prayed (adapting Is. 55.10) that God's blessing would be poured out on the Corinthians as a result of their generous giving.

Paul described the cyclical effect that occurs in giving. Thanksgiving to God supplies the needs of the saints, who give to believers out of their supply and mercy. The believers, in thanksgiving, gave out of their abundance to others, who in turn are thankful to God.

God's indescribable gift is restored relationship and eternal life through the death and resurrection of His Son.

INSIGHTS

Although Paul's sowing and reaping analogy perhaps resonated more clearly with first century readers than twenty-first century readers, the concept is still valid. Many people hoard what they have and only give grudgingly. They are later surprised when they find few people to help them in their own time of need. All we have belongs to God, who graciously allows us to be stewards of His belongings. In our role as stewards, God expects us to meet the needs of those around us within the ability with which He has blessed us. When we give generously as God intends, we also reap the rewards both here and in the life to come.

1. Giving is an important part of the Christian life. Though the focus is often on money, we also have other resources from which we can give. Meals for the infirmed, a place to sleep, some of our time, and the expertise of our talents are other common areas we can give from. Where and what are you being asked to give? Can God count on you to give cheerfully, even when you may have had other plans for what God is asking you to give?

2. Have you experienced a time when God met your needs through the generosity of other believers? Has God used you to meet the needs of others who are suffering? How are both these (receiving in need and giving to those in need) a reflection of God's redeeming work through His Son's life, death and resurrection?

2 CORINTHIANS, CHAPTER 10

BACKGROUND

A fortress that sat on a 1,857 foot high hill protected ancient Corinth. This imposing stronghold would have been difficult for any enemy to overcome in order to take control of the city. The imagery of war, strongholds, towers and captives was often used in ancient writings.

The Greeks especially paid great attention to rhetorical styles in Paul's time. Manuals were written about how to give or write various types of communication (persuasive, informative, etc.). Those who did not follow the conventions were viewed as ineffective.

OVERVIEW

Paul and Timothy co-authored this letter to the Corinthians (2 Cor. 1.1). *I, Paul* meant that he was speaking for himself and was not including Timothy in the following comments.

Paul's critics had accused him of being meek when visiting the Corinthian believers and bold only in his writings to them.

Paul wanted the Corinthian believers to deal with his critics so he would not have to be stern (bold) with them when he visited.

Though Paul lived in the world, he did not do battle as the world did. Instead he used the divine weapons God made available to him. *Arguments* were human thoughts, which needed to come under the control of Christ. *Strongholds* and *every pretense (high thing)* were the people and plans that did not align with the gospel message that Paul taught.

In the context of Paul's current subject, belonging to Christ meant more than having placed one's faith in Him. Paul was implying being a servant or disciple.

Though Jesus had given Paul authority, that authority was for edification, not destruction. *Edification* means building up while *destruction* means tearing down. Paul was concerned about correcting the abuses that had occurred in the Corinthian church. His aim was not to destroy the church.

Paul's critics compared his writings to his speeches and perceived a difference; he wrote with boldness he did not possess when he spoke. It may have been that Paul was a more effective writer than speaker. It may also have been that Paul did not follow the conventions of his day. He did plant numerous churches while on his missionary journeys, so he could not have been completely ineffective in his speaking. It may simply have been that his critics tried to discount him by whatever means they could. Regardless of the differences between Paul's speaking and writing, he intended to show the Corinthian believers that what he did in person was not inconsistent with what he wrote in his letters.

Teachers in the Mediterranean region competed for students and their fees. One method of attracting students was by comparing oneself to other teachers. Paul refused to be drawn into such tactics. Paul would limit his boasting to the ministry God had given; that ministry included the Corinthians. Paul implies that his critics, on the other hand, were not boasting in work they had done but in work others (Paul) had done before they arrived.

Regions beyond you may have referred to Spain where Paul hoped to go (Rom. 15.24).

Paul's own boasting had been motivated by the need to defend himself against false accusations. He preferred to boast about the work of the Lord and recognized that what truly mattered was the praise of God.

INSIGHTS

In a culture that stresses the importance of doing only those things that feel good at the moment, personal discipline is not very popular. Paul's encouragement to *bring every thought into captivity to the obedience of Christ* flies in the face of our culture's value, yet it has great value in God's eyes. It is only through the hard work of taking thoughts captive and engaging in other forms of self-discipline that we are able to free ourselves of many sins and temptations that decrease our effectiveness as Christian witnesses and servants of God who readily seek to be obedient to Him.

1. Just as Paul experienced, God makes available to believers divine weapons that allow us to do battle on a spiritual level. When faced with a hardship, trial or suffering, do you employ the weapons God has given or fall back on worldly weapons to see you through? What can you do to gain confidence in the weapons and authority God gives believers through Jesus Christ?

2. In an age of red carpet celebrities, sports superstars and larger-than-life movie stars, we see and hear all kinds of boasting in personal ability and accomplishment. How is boasting in God different? Why is it important to recognize God as the source for all we have to boast about?

2 Corinthians, Chapter 11

BACKGROUND

Paul listed a variety of trials he endured from the time of his conversion to the time of his letter (vv. 25-28). Luke recorded some of those events in the book of Acts (beaten 16.23; stoned 14.19; in danger from the Greeks 17.5-10; in peril of his countrymen 9.23-4). Other events are not recorded in either Acts or Paul's own writings. Second Corinthians was written prior to Paul's arrest by the Jews, so the three shipwrecks he mentioned are in addition to the one he experienced on his way to Rome.

OVERVIEW

Though Paul believed boasting in oneself was foolishness (a statement he repeats throughout this chapter), he did so because the circumstances warranted it. He thanked the Corinthian believers for putting up with him in this.

As the Corinthian believers' spiritual father, Paul felt a rightful jealously toward them. Through his teaching they had been betrothed to Christ and he wanted them to remain chaste virgins. In other words, uncorrupted by false teachings. He was afraid, however, that they would be deceived just as Eve had been by the evil intent of the serpent. The Greek word translated as simplicity has also been translated as singleness and sincerity. The Corinthians had a sincere singleness of heart toward Jesus that Paul did not want to be corrupted by false teachings.

Another Jesus would be someone who did not encompass all Jesus did: man but not God; crucified but not risen. Likewise a different gospel would lack grace, focusing instead on the law, or emphasizing works and negating faith.

Teachers commonly charged fees for their training. Paul refrained from this practice so as not to be a burden to the people and not to appear to be teaching only for personal gain. It is unlikely that Paul literally meant he robbed other churches. Rather, in the heat of his argument he more likely meant he was supported in his efforts by the contributions from already established churches.

Paul dismissed the idea that he did not charge for his teaching because he did not love the Corinthians.

The false teachers were transforming (disguising/masquerading) themselves as Christ's apostles. Since Satan himself could masquerade as an angel of light, it should not be surprising that his minions could masquerade as servants of righteousness.

Not according to the Lord meant the Lord's standard. Jesus was the model of humility and had not engaged in boasting.

Paul worried that the Corinthians were not only listening to (putting up with) the false teaching, but that they were willing to become enslaved, consumed, burdened, ruled over and insulted by the false message.

Paul's commitment to not receiving personal gain from his preaching and teaching was accompanied by a long list of trials he had endured in order to share the good news.

Paul repeated his aversion to boasting, stating that he would boast in his weakness rather than in his strength as the others did.

Having to escape Damascus in a basket (Acts 9.25) was the example Paul used to show his weakness.

INSIGHTS

Paul's statement that Satan can disguise himself as an angel of light is worth remembering today. Satan is a cunning deceiver who will go to great lengths to dissuade anyone he is able to stray from the tenets of Christianity and the power of Jesus Christ. Just as Satan convinced Eve she would not die if she ate the fruit from the Tree of the Knowledge of Good and Evil, he attempts to convince us that what God has said to be true is not really true. Like Eve, who discovered that death was the real consequence (Gen. 3), we will suffer the consequences of sin if we allow the angel of light to deceive us.

1. Paul was willing to endure many trials and suffer much in order to take every opportunity to share the gospel with unbelievers and encourage believers. What are you willing to endure to share the good news of Christ with those who need to hear it? What comfort(s) might God be calling you to give up for Him?

2. Paul was very concerned that the people sharing mistruths about Christ would persuade the Corinthian believers who would, as a result, end up living in bondage to lies. How can we protect ourselves from believing lies and mistruths about Christ? How does reading God's word daily help to instill truth in our hearts?

2 Corinthians, Chapter 12

BACKGROUND

Paul was not alone in his *otherworldly* experience. God met Moses on Mt. Sinai (Ex. 19.19-20). Moses and Elijah spoke with Christ on the hillside while Peter, James and John saw the glorified Christ (Matt. 17.1-8). John saw heavenly visions (Rev.). The visions were never an end in themselves but served to bring glory to God and draw His people to Him.

OVERVIEW

The *man in Christ* is thought to be Paul himself. It was considered prideful to discuss great honor coming on oneself and so was often done in the third person.

Fourteen years earlier would have been approximately 42-44 A.D, after Paul's conversion and prior to his commissioning for his first missionary trip.

The precise meaning of the *third heaven* is not known. Many believe the three heavens commonly referred to were: 1) the atmosphere, 2) where the stars and moon exist, and 3) where God resides.

Paul did not include details of his vision but communicated enough to let his readers know what he saw was beyond description. Paul mentions his vision of heaven only here. He is careful to make sure the focus stays on God rather than being turned to himself through boasting about what he had experienced.

The nature of Paul's *thorn in the flesh* is unknown. Several possibilities exist. Flesh may mean Paul's body, in which case he was afflicted by a physical ailment, possibly poor eyesight (Gal. 4.15). Flesh might refer to humanity's fallen nature. In this case Paul may have referred to a repeated temptation. Flesh may also have been used figuratively. If so, Paul was speaking about the persecution or opposition he repeatedly faced. Most scholars believe Paul suffered from a physical affliction.

Though Paul repeatedly prayed for relief from his ailment, God chose not to heal him. Paul came to recognize that his ailment provided a weakness through which Christ could work and God could show Himself strong. As a result, Paul was able to rejoice in his own affliction and weakness.

Paul's ministry in Corinth had included all the miracles and supernatural occurrences that had accompanied the other apostles' work and verified his authority as an apostle.

Paul had given the Corinthian church preferential treatment by not seeking his personal support from them. He used a bit of irony and sarcasm by asking for their forgiveness for such treatment.

Paul first stopped at Corinth during his second missionary journey. Scholars have debated whether there was an actual second visit before Paul wrote this letter or if Paul counted his intent and inability to come as the second. In any case, Paul was ready for another visit and promised to be no more burdensome on that trip than he was on the first.

Paul used sarcasm to show the folly of his critics' arguments. Titus was a man of high standing and had not been sent by Paul to collect what Paul had not claimed for himself.

Paul was fearful of finding the Corinthian believers indulging themselves in sin (*not as I wish*) and would therefore have to discipline them (*not as you wish*). He would mourn if he found them involved in a myriad of sinful behaviors.

INSIGHTS

In a culture that emphasizes *going it alone, pulling yourself up by your bootstraps* or *trust no one,* our being weak that the strength of Christ might be evident is not very popular. Because we were designed in God's image, we were made to be in relationship with others, to share our burdens, seek others' assistance and offer the same to them. Being completely reliant upon one's self is a myth and unachievable. Paul recognized that any ability he had came from God. Therefore, any means of glorifying God was good, even if that opportunity came from his own suffering and trials.

1. During his lifetime, Paul never experienced the healing he prayed for. God used Paul's affliction to remind Paul of God's presence, strength and provision in his life. Is there an ongoing affliction, trial or burden you have prayed God would take away that He has chosen not to? In your resulting suffering and weakness, how is God showing His strength and mercy on your behalf?

2. Paul was fearful he would come and find the Corinthian believers embroiled in sin. Do you attempt to live your life in such a way that you will not be surprised, embarrassed or fearful of anyone seeing you? How can you intentionally and transparently live your life in a way that reflects the Gospel?

2 Corinthians, Chapter 13

BACKGROUND

Both the Old Testament and the New Testament required at least two witnesses to verify the truth of a statement given as evidence against another. Most references include the phrase *two or three witnesses* (Deut. 17.6; 19.15; Matt. 18.16; 1 Tim. 5.19).

OVERVIEW

Paul repeated his desire that he wanted the Corinthians to heed the warnings of his letter and address the sin some members of the church were engaging in (12.20; 13.2, 10). If they would not do so before he arrived, Paul would take on the task himself.

Paul assured the Corinthians that their demand for proof that he had *Christ speaking in (through) me* would be met when he arrived. Some of Paul's critics thought Christ, who was strong, could not be speaking through Paul, who was weak. Paul pointed to the irony of weakness in Christ. Christ appeared to be weak when He died on the cross. In reality He was doing the work of God by God's strength. Likewise, Paul and all believers were also weak in their own abilities, but faith in Christ made the power of God available to carry on His work.

Paul encouraged the Corinthian believers to test themselves to see if they truly had Christ in them. He was concerned that they were not applying the same standards to themselves and to Paul.

Paul was not as concerned that the Corinthians' actions justified

Paul and his message as he was that they would choose to do what was right.

As Paul closed his letter, he shared his desire that the believers love one another, be united in their efforts and live in peace.

A *holy kiss* was used to greet friends and family members in much the same way a handshake or hug is used in Western culture. A kiss of greeting is still used in some cultures today and is quite prevalent in the Eastern and Russian Orthodox churches.

Paul's closing benediction also included the means of living righteously; the grace, love and communion of the triune God would solve many of the Corinthian believers' problems.

INSIGHTS

Paul was willing to say the hard things in order that the Corinthian believers might be edified and grow in their maturity and understanding of Jesus Christ. Likewise, we should be willing to say the hard words to fellow believers that they too may grow in Christ. Today's culture encourages us to *mind our own business* and *leave well enough alone*, but sometimes such an approach causes us to miss opportunities for God to use us in the life of another. God created us with a strong need for fellowship. True intimacy in relationships is reached when we are willing to confront another for his/her own well-being.

1. How does acknowledging your human weakness and embracing God's strength in you serve God's purposes of spreading His good news to the unbelieving and hurting world? Why would God want you to be strong in Him rather than in your own strength? How have you seen God work during your times of weakness?

2. Paul encouraged the Corinthian church to examine themselves to see if they were living in the faith. How can we accurately and adequately live out the faith today? How is regular self-examination one of several spiritual practices that can help us avoid the temptations of sin and falling victim to the lies and mistruths of false teachers?

FIRST THESSALONIANS

While on his second missionary journey, Paul stopped in Thessalonica to preach the good news of Jesus Christ, just as he had been doing throughout his journey. While some were persuaded by Paul's message, others became jealous and fearful. They incited a riot that forced Paul and his companion, Silas, to flee (Acts 17.1-11).

As spiritual father to the new believers in Thessalonica, Paul was concerned about their welfare and ability to withstand those who had caused him to flee. As Paul records in his letter, he was relieved to hear the believers had maintained their newfound faith, were growing in love for each other and had good memories of Paul's visit (1 Thess. 3.6).

Paul wrote 1 Thessalonians to encourage the new believers, further teach them about the faith and answer questions about how to live out their faith. He also responded to attacks on his character and integrity that had been leveled by Jewish opponents.

First Thessalonians is believed by many scholars to be the first or second surviving letter written by Paul. It can be divided into two parts. In chapters 1-3, Paul shared his heart on matters of the faith, encouraging and affirming his readers. In chapters 4-5, Paul addressed some specific issues that dealt with living out the faith in an appropriate manner.

1 Thessalonians, Chapter 1

BACKGROUND

Thessalonica is one of several cities in the Roman region of Macedonia that Paul visited in order to preach the good news of Christ. The city would have been appealing to Paul because of its strategic location on both land and sea routes. A strong body of believers in the city would have greatly facilitated the spread of the gospel throughout the Roman Empire and beyond.

OVERVIEW

Paul opened his letter to the Thessalonians in the manner standard for the times: author, recipient, and salutation. Though Paul mentioned Silvanus and Timothy, Paul was the author.

Silvanus is the Latin name of Silas. Jewish parents who were also Roman citizens often gave their children similarly sounding Jewish and Latin names.

The phrase *your election by God* meant the Thessalonians had chosen to accept God's invitation to be counted among His people. As God's people, three virtues became evident: faith, love and hope. Note the virtues are not listed by themselves but each is a part of and directed toward God. The work of faith is repentance. The labor of love is serving others. The patience (endurance) of hope is found in Christ's return.

The Thessalonians journey to faith had already been marked by trial. They had heard Paul's message in the midst of great opposition. Yet the joy that comes only from the Holy Spirit had settled so strongly in them that those in the surrounding areas were noticing their faith. In fact, the Thessalonians' rejection of a multitude of idols for the one true

God was so strong, travelers in the region were sharing the amazing events with Paul without his promptings.

INSIGHTS

The gospel message had taken so strong a hold on the initially small group of believers in Thessalonica that they could not help but be witnesses to the redeeming message they had heard. Likewise, we should seek to realize the magnitude of the gifts God has given each of us as believers. Our lives should then reflect the outpouring of God's love, grace, redemption and peace so that those around us will want to hear about Jesus. When temptation, trials and difficulties threaten our witness, we can turn to God for strength and wisdom. He desires to equip us for all we face and sometimes is just waiting for us to ask for His help.

1. Paul thanked God for the Thessalonian's faith, love, and endurance inspired by their hope in the Lord Jesus Christ. Is there someone in your life that shares the same heart for Christ as the Thessalonians? Have you thanked God for their impact on your life? If possible, consider encouraging them with a letter of appreciation for the impact they have had on your faith-walk.

2. Paul commended the Thessalonians for being imitators of the Lord, and, in spite of severe suffering, they welcomed the message with joy. Can you think of a time when you were ridiculed, outcast, or suffered for being an imitator of Christ? How did you handle that difficult time?

1 Thessalonians, Chapter 2

BACKGROUND

Paul and Silas had been beaten and thrown in jail during their stay in Philippi as a result of freeing a slave girl from the grips of demon possession (Acts 16.16-24). Paul's trials did not dissuade him from continuing on his mission to preach the good news of Christ to those who had not yet heard.

OVERVIEW

Paul's determination to preach the good news of Christ in the face of opposition was a testimony to Paul's unshakable faith in the truth of what he preached. That truth came from God and had not been contrived in any manner. He had not attempted to realize any personal gain by teaching erroneously, with impure motives, or through the use of trickery.

Paul had been commissioned by God to preach the gospel and worked solely for His approval.

Paul's message should be taken at face value. He had not used flattery or used the message to hide greed. Both were common practices for teachers of his day.

It was common practice for teachers to seek or expect payment for imparting their wisdom. Paul had chosen not to engage in this practice. Instead he had used other means to support himself.

Paul's image of nursing mothers portrayed his feelings toward the believers in Thessalonica; feelings of gentleness, love and even a willingness to give up his own life. Later Paul used the image of a father—encouraging, comforting and concerned—to explain his urgings that the Thessalonians live lives worthy of God.

Paul had worked as an artisan (many believe he was a tent maker) in order to not be a burden to the Thessalonians. The workday generally began at sunrise and, depending on the trade, could finish in early afternoon. That would have left much of the afternoon and early evening for Paul to focus more completely on evangelism.

Paul praised the Thessalonians for recognizing the truth contained in the message he preached.

The Thessalonians had imitated the virtues of their fellow Judean believers and suffered as a result of opposition to the gospel of Christ. Such suffering should not have been a surprise, since God's prophets, Son and Paul himself had suffered because of the message they delivered.

Having been taken (torn) away literally means orphaned. Paul bemoaned the separation that existed between himself and his beloved spiritual children. He desired to see them but had been prevented from doing so. Those who opposed Paul tried to convince the new believers that Paul had actually abandoned them by promising to come and then delaying the visit.

A crown was a wreath given to the winner of an athletic competition. Paul looked forward to the satisfaction he would experience when the Thessalonians joined him in the presence of Christ.

INSIGHTS

Paul was clear about his mission – sharing the gospel of Christ with unbelievers – and certain of the means he would employ to do so – ensuring he did not burden those to whom he ministered. We can be just as certain about the mission God has established for us and the means through which we are to achieve it. God calls each of us to actively work in His unfolding plan. He has gifted and equipped each of us and is well pleased in our efforts to obediently fulfill our part. One of the rewards to doing so is a greater sense of fulfillment than is achieved through any other type of work.

1. Paul wrote that he, Silas, and Timothy had pure motives and spoke to the Thessalonians as men approved by God to be entrusted with the gospel. They were not trying to please men but God who tests our hearts. Do you ever struggle with being a person-pleaser versus a God-pleaser? What would your life look like if obeying, honoring, and pleasing God were your priorities?

2. Paul described how he and his companions delighted in not only sharing the gospel with the Thessalonians but sharing their very lives as well. They toiled and worked hard day and night in order to not be a burden to anyone while they preached the gospel. Are you sharing your life with other believers more than just at the coffee hour on Sunday after church? In love, are you serving with and for one another?

1 Thessalonians, Chapter 3

BACKGROUND

Timothy was the son of a Greek (i.e. Gentile) father and a Jewish mother. Lack of any reference to his father suggests he may have died when Timothy was an infant. His mother, Eunice, and grandmother, Lois, raised him. Paul shared the gospel with the family on his first missionary journey. Seven years later, during Paul's second trip, Timothy had grown to manhood and it was suggested he was well suited for missionary work. Timothy then accompanied Paul and Silas as they continued on their missionary journey.

OVERVIEW

Because Paul had to leave Thessalonica earlier than he would have liked, the new believers were left without any leadership. Paul sent Timothy to Thessalonica to further establish and encourage them in their newfound faith.

Because Timothy was not as mature in his faith as his mentor, Paul included an endorsement of Timothy as a brother in the faith, a minister of God and a laborer in the gospel.

Paul had taught that suffering was a part of the Christian experience. Therefore, he suggested the Thessalonians should not be disheartened when such events occurred.

As new believers, Paul was particularly aware of the risk the Thessalonians faced in light of Satan's attempts to dissuade and discourage them. He was overjoyed when Timothy returned with the good report of the Thessalonians' steadfast faith.

Paul prayed for the Thessalonians, both thanking God for the work He was doing in them and asking that their faith might continue to grow and be strengthened.

Now may our God introduced both a prayer and a desire for some event to occur. In this case, Paul prayed God would make the way clear for him to visit the Thessalonians, the Lord would continue to grow in them as evidenced by their love for one another and those not yet believers, and that they would stand without faults, holy before God.

INSIGHTS

Just as Paul desired that the Thessalonians mature in their faith, so we always have room to grow in our faith. A desire to mature, a heart that is open to teaching, and a plan to study God's Word will help facilitate that growth. It can be helpful to pick a topic, such as a Biblical book, particular subject (love, money), or discipline (fasting, solitude) we would like to cultivate. Set aside time each week to focus on what the Bible says about the chosen topic. Other resources, such as commentaries, devotionals, and spiritual retreats can be helpful. Prayers for discernment, understanding and wisdom during the process are essential.

1. Paul described the Thessalonians as the crown in which he would glory in the presence Jesus. Paul also said the Thessalonians were his glory and joy. Is there anyone in your life you can describe as passionately as Paul did the Thessalonians? Have you shared the gospel with anyone who has been restored, renewed, and/or transformed by it?

2. Paul prayed that, through the Lord, his readers' love would increase and flow over for one another and their hearts would be strengthened so they would be blameless and holy in the presence of God. Who can you pray this powerful prayer for today?

1 Thessalonians, Chapter 4

BACKGROUND

Falling asleep was an expression meaning someone had died. It is similar to modern day expressions such as *passed away*, *pass on*, or *gone to be with the Lord*.

OVERVIEW

Having praised and encouraged the Thessalonians because of their steadfastness in faith, Paul then moved to doctrinal issues that needed attention.

Greek and Roman religious practices often included sexual intercourse with prostitutes and the Romans had few sexual boundaries outside of religion. Since these practices had been accepted as normal for the Gentiles, those new to the faith likely were tempted in this area. Paul urged his readers to restrain from sexual immorality and reserve sexual practices for the bonds of marriage.

His own vessel was a person's body. God had created each person; therefore, each believer should treat his/her body with the reverence and honor deserving of God.

It was a common Jewish belief that having premarital sex committed adultery against the person's future spouse. Paul warned that God would be the one to judge or take revenge against those who engaged in such practices.

In Greek, *defrauding his brother* carries a sense of robbing or cheating someone. Sexual immorality was not only a sinful act between two people but also stole something from someone else (the current or future spouse).

Paul used *uncleanness* for the opposite of *holiness*. Anyone who engaged in immoral sexual activity was not holy and therefore rejected God and the Holy Spirit who resides in each believer.

The Thessalonians had a good reputation for loving others. Paul did not want them to take that reputation for granted or stop extending love to those around them but to continue to grow as God and the Holy Spirit directed.

Leading a quiet life referred to inner quietness or peace rather than limited activity. Paul also wanted his readers to refrain from meddling in other people's affairs and to avoid being a drain on other people because they chose not to work. These things would do a great deal in allowing the believer to be a good witness to those who did not yet know the good news of Christ.

Believers in Christ had a hope that pagans did not have: death only temporarily separated believers from one another. For pagans, death was a permanent separation from God and each other.

Though the Thessalonians had heard Paul's teaching on death and Christ's second coming, they needed to be reminded that those who died before Jesus returned did not lose out on participating in His glory. They, in fact, had gone on ahead of those who were still alive; both would be reunited when Christ descended from heaven.

INSIGHTS

Paul called the Thessalonians to continue growing in their ability to love one another. Just as they had room for continued improvement, so do we. God wants His people to be holy just as He is holy (Lev. 11.44-45; 1 Pet. 1.15-16). Doing so is a process (called sanctification) that takes one's whole life. As we grow in our understanding of who God is and our desire to please Him, we can sometimes become frustrated when we fail to see progress in ourselves. God is faithful to those who genuinely desire to grow and will send the Holy Spirit to work in us to that end. Progress can sometimes seem exceedingly slow, but do not lose heart. God *is* at work!

1. Paul reminded the Thessalonians that God did not call them to be impute but to live holy lives. Whoever rejected the instruction also rejected God who gives the Holy Spirit. Is there something you are watching, reading, or participating in that is preventing you from living a pure and holy life? Is there any area of your life that you need the Holy Spirit to help you clean up?

2. Paul told his readers that their ambitions should include quietly minding their own business and working diligently with their hands so that their daily lives might win the respect of outsiders. What are your ambitions? Do you strive to gain the respect of others through what you say and do?

1 Thessalonians, Chapter 5

BACKGROUND

The Day of the Lord was an Old Testament phrase that readers of the Hebrew Scriptures would have been familiar with. Generally the term refers to the final judgment that will occur when Jesus returns. The phrase could also refer to any period during which God's judgment was cast upon the earth. Some of the Old Testament prophecies concerning the Day of the Lord have been fulfilled, while others remain to be fulfilled.

OVERVIEW

But concerning was generally used to introduce a new topic. Believers could be certain of Jesus' second coming but were uncertain as to when it would occur.

Paul's *day of the Lord* referred to the second coming of Christ and the judgment that would accompany it. Just as a thief in the night does not announce where he will strike, so the Lord will not proclaim when He is coming before He returns. To unbelievers, the Lord's coming will be like the first pains of a woman in labor – sudden and unexpected.

Unlike unbelievers, the Thessalonians knew Christ would come a second time. They might not know precisely when the event would occur but would not be taken by surprise when it did come to pass.

Let us not sleep referred to being asleep spiritually (not being aware of God's will) rather than physically. Being spiritually awake meant being aware of what was to come and preparing for it to come to pass at anytime.

Paul equated being sober and watchful with living a disciplined life.

For the second time in his first letter to the Thessalonians, Paul referred to the basic necessities of the Christian life: faith, love and hope. Breastplates and helmets were essential pieces of armor when going into battle. The three basic necessities should be treated as just as essential to the Christian life.

Though God's wrath will be evident on the day of the Lord, it will not be directed at believers. Believers are protected by God's mercy and promise of salvation.

The Thessalonian church was filled with relatively new believers and leadership may not have been readily apparent. Nevertheless, Paul admonished his readers to submit to the church leadership. The pronoun *those* is plural and indicates the Thessalonian church was led by more than one person, following the pattern of the churches in Jerusalem and Antioch.

Some within the body of believers were not exhibiting the most Christ-like behavior. Paul counseled his readers to address those issues and to ensure, in the process, that they themselves were not responding inappropriately.

Praying without ceasing meant regularly and diligently, not constantly.

Quenching the Spirit was achieved by resisting His influence and direction.

Testing all things involved evaluating them against the dictates of scripture. For those issues not covered directly by God's Word, the counsel of godly men and women can be used.

When Paul called believers to be blameless he meant individuals should repent of and seek forgiveness for their sin, as well as be in good standing with those around them.

INSIGHTS

Paul exhorted his readers to rejoice always, pray continually and give thanks in all things (not for all things). Such urging can seem impossible. How can we rejoice when trials are intense? How can we pray without ceasing? How can we rejoice when circumstances seem dire? God does not ask us to do what is impossible. Sometimes we can rejoice when it seems inappropriate because we know God will bring good out of the current difficulties (Gen. 50.20). At other times, we can offer micro prayers that are answered in unbelievable ways (Neh.2.4-8). At still other times, God God orders dire circumstances in ways we can't imagine (Rom. 8.28).

1. Paul's instructions included being self-controlled, putting on faith and love as a breastplate, and donning the hope of salvation as a helmet. Can you think of practical examples of how putting on faith, hope and love will help you maintain self-control in your everyday life?

2. Consider having Paul's final instructions in verses 12-22 printed, made as "house rules," or challenge yourself to memorize them! As you read the verses, ask yourself if you respect those who work hard, live in peace with each other, and help the weak? Are you patient with everyone? Are you kind to everyone? Are you joyful always? Do you pray continually and give thanks in all circumstances? Do you hold on to the good and avoid every kind of evil? Finally, pray and ask the God of peace to sanctify you through and through that your whole spirit, soul, and body be kept blameless at the coming of our Lord Jesus Christ.

SECOND THESSALONIANS

Paul wrote his second letter to the Thessalonians to combat some misinformation they had been given about the second coming of Christ. Paul wanted these new believers to live in the freedom of their faith, yet not be deceived into living anything less than God-honoring lives.

Second Thessalonians can be divided into three parts corresponding to its three chapters. In the first chapter, Paul encouraged the Thessalonians to remain faithful in the face of the persecution they faced. In the second chapter he clarified expectations about the day of the Lord. The final chapter is an exhortation to continued faithfulness.

2 THESSALONIANS, CHAPTER 1

BACKGROUND

Just as precisely when the Lord will return is unknown, so is how He will return. Several references portray Jesus as returning on clouds (Lk. 21.27; Rev. 1.7). Others suggest he will be riding a horse (Rev. 19.11). Another picture is more warrior-like as Jesus returns with His mighty angels surrounded by blazing fire (2 Thess. 1.6-8).

OVERVIEW

Paul began his letter with praise for the Thessalonian church. They had not only endured persecution but also allowed their faith to grow in the midst of all they were experiencing. Such genuine maturity was well worth boasting about and Paul did so whenever he had a chance.

Suffering and tribulation were to be expected. Those who endured it well would be rewarded by God and see His judgment on the wrongdoers come to pass. One of the rewards is rest – freedom from persecution, trouble and tribulation.

Those who do not know God was a phrase meaning those who rejected God. It did not mean those who had never heard of God. The phrase is modified by the next phrase *those who do not obey the gospel*. The punishment was not annihilation but destruction or eternal separation from God.

Paul prayed the Thessalonians would remain steadfast in their faith, giving continuing testimony to the glory of God.

INSIGHTS

Paul did two things for the new believers in Thessalonica. He praised them for their steadfast faith and prayed that they would continue to testify to God's glory. These are two things we can do for those around us today. New believers especially, but all believers as well, benefit from our sincere praise of the ways in which they are steadfast in their faith. Likewise, all believers benefit from our prayers. Even when we don't know the specifics of what to pray for, we can pray that their behavior, actions, words and deeds would continually bring glory to God. God will honor such prayers and work in the lives of those around us.

1. Paul told the Thessalonians he boasted about their perseverance and faith displayed throughout the persecution and trials they endured. Could Paul boast about your perseverance and faith through the trials you are enduring today? If not, what are some practical things (prayer, a time of fasting, repentance, accountability group, etc.) you can do to help strengthen your faith that would allow you to persevere more confidently?

2. Paul was certain that God's justice would prevail. Are you just as confident? Do you trust God's justice in light of those who trouble you? Do you trust Him for your relief and provision in times of trouble?

2 Thessalonians, Chapter 2

BACKGROUND

False teaching was circulating through Thessalonica that the day of the Lord had already come and was responsible for the tribulation the believers were then experiencing. This left some believers thinking God had passed them by because their faith had not measured up to God's standards.

OVERVIEW

Paul stated that false teaching was being passed off as his and circulated by prophecy, word of mouth and letter. The believers were to guard against these false teachings and stand firm in what they knew to be true. Specific events would take place before the Lord returned, including a falling away and the appearance of the man of sin, commonly called the Antichrist. Scholars have generally interpreted *falling away* in one of two ways. It may be spiritually oriented and refer to a general rebellion against God. Or it may be more physically oriented and mean the rapture (gathering of all believers to Christ) will occur prior to the ascent to power by the man of sin.

The man of sin would lead people away from God by passing himself off as god and demanding people worship him. Some interpreters believe the man of sin will stand in the re-erected physical temple in Jerusalem. Others believe temple means the church and the man of sin will attempt to redirect worship of God to himself.

It is uncertain as to the exact meaning of *what is restraining*. It is used in two senses: first in reference to some type of evil that will increase in the world and second, as one (perhaps the Holy Spirit) who suppresses the lawlessness that is yet to come.

The extreme power the lawless one will have will come from Satan. Although his power will appear indomitable, Christ will have no difficulty in subduing him.

The man of sin will deceive many who would not receive the gospel of Christ and who will ultimately be condemned.

Paul was thankful for the Thessalonian believers. They knew the truth and would experience salvation even as the work of sanctification was continuing in them.

The Thessalonians had received the truth of God through Paul's personal teaching and through his writings. He encouraged them to stand fast in the faith they knew to be true.

Paul finished this section by praying the Thessalonians would experience the peace and hope of Jesus and the Father in their hearts and in all they did.

INSIGHTS

The deception Paul warned the Thessalonians to be on guard against is just as strong today. In the name of God the Father and Jesus Christ, many people attempt to explain the scriptures in ways other than God intended. These people attempt to realize personal gain, whether power, finances or self-importance, by reinterpreting the scriptures to meet their own ends. It takes discernment, knowledge of the scriptures, strong Christian fellowship and a continuing intimacy with God to discern the attempts to lead us away from God. As we continue to turn to God, He will see us through the deceptions.

1. Satan and the lawless man will one day work together in an attempt to usurp God's rule and reign over the entire universe. While we do not know when this will occur, there is plenty of evidence that Satan is at work in our world today. Are you fully confident in God and the victory He has already won through Christ's sacrifice on the cross? Are you able to find peace in God despite the turmoil, unrest, and mayhem around the world?

2. Paul challenged the Thessalonians to stand firm in their faith and hold onto the truth he had taught them. Paul recognized that people perished because they refused to love the truth and so be saved. Can you think of any false teaching or doctrine today that is deceiving many from loving the truth and being saved? How can you stand firm in God's Word?

2 Thessalonians, Chapter 3

BACKGROUND

Jesus outlined a series of steps to be taken when discipline of a disobedient believer was necessary. First was a meeting with the offender. Second was a meeting with the offender and another church member. Third was an announcement to the congregation who would encourage the offender to repent. Lastly, the congregation treated the offender like an unbeliever. Each step was designed to draw the offender to repentance and the process did not proceed to following steps once the sinner repented (Matt. 18.15-17).

OVERVIEW

Just as Paul prayed for the believers in Thessalonica, he requested that they pray for him, especially that the gospel would spread rapidly. The word *glorified* includes a sense of being successful in a continuing manner that works toward an overall goal. The opposition Paul experienced in Thessalonica and other cities he had visited motivated his prayer for deliverance from unreasonable and wicked men. Not everyone who heard Paul's message believed, with some opposing Paul so strongly he was run out of town.

Paul's confidence in the Thessalonians' ability to do as he commanded was not rooted in a desire to be powerful but in the knowledge that he was an intermediary for the Lord, who would provide the means to carry out His will.

Paul's command given in the *name of the Lord Jesus Christ* means Paul was acting as Jesus' representative.

Disorderly (unruly) may have meant idle. Paul was instructing the Thessalonians to have limited fellowship with those who were disobedient. Paul used his own work ethic as an example of what others should do. His primary objective in working while preaching was to avoid being a burden to those around him. Paul could have followed the common practice of requiring payment for his teaching. By not doing so, Paul felt he was:

- ensuring nothing would hinder the spread of the gospel;
- eliminating any accusations that he was using the gospel for personal gain;
- and setting the standard for how others should go about spreading the gospel.

It is interesting to note Paul was not suggesting that he needed to entirely support himself through his own efforts while on his missionary journeys. A portion of Paul's support came from already established believers (i.e. churches), and he supplemented the rest through his own labor.

The strong emphasis on charity that was a part of Judaism did not extend to those capable of work but who refused to do so. Believers were not obligated to support such people; they were to eat the bread of their own labor. Paul used a strong word, *command*, in his instructions that the church should discipline those who could, but would not work.

Paul recognized that idleness could be a breeding ground for sin and felt that much of the disorderly conduct and meddling would disappear if people filled their time with productive, meaningful work.

Paul was careful to ensure that his words could not be misinterpreted as a recommendation to cease *doing good*, i.e. discontinue providing charity to those in need.

The limited fellowship with those who were idle without reason did not make them enemies but brothers who were being disciplined.

Paul closed by praying for both the peace and grace of the Lord, in which the solutions to the believers' difficulties would be found.

INSIGHTS

Breaking fellowship with a disobedient believer is not a punishment that seeks to gain retribution for the offense. Rather its purpose is to draw the offender to repentance and back into a right relationship with God. It is hoped that treating a disobedient believer as an unbeliever will create a desire to return to the fellowship s/he enjoyed prior to the offense and cause repentance to occur. Breaking fellowship with the disobedient believer does not mean having nothing to do with him/her. It does mean limiting contact, not confiding to the same previous level and yet still showing the unconditional love of Jesus.

1. Paul was able to share the gospel with the Thessalonians and other Gentiles because of the support he had from various believers and churches. How are you participating in the spread of the gospel? Is God calling you to support a missionary or mission organization? Is He calling you to take a step of faith and share the good news with an unbelieving friend?

2. Paul emphasized the importance of working diligently and avoiding the idle brother. He also urged the busybodies to settle down, earn the bread they eat, and not tire of doing what is right. Why is this important to the spread of the Gospel? Would your friends or family consider you a hard worker? Do your friends and acquaintances work tirelessly at doing what is right?

ROMANS

No one is quite certain how or when the church in Rome was started. It is possible the church began shortly after Pentecost when Roman Jews returned home with the amazing testimony of the life of Christ and the power of the Holy Spirit. However or whenever the church started, it soon gained traction and began to spread throughout the Roman Empire.

During his third missionary journey, with plans to return to the church in Jerusalem before heading to Rome and Spain, Paul wrote his letter to the church in Rome. Though well established, the church lacked instructional material that gave them direction on how to live the Christian life. Paul provided a theological exposition that is logically, thoughtfully and clearly presented.

In the letter, Paul explained God's plan for salvation. He began with the bad news that all people have sinned and are in need of a savior. He then moved to the good news that God did not wait for humanity to cease sinning before setting in place a plan that would make salvation available to all who chose to believe in His Son. Then Paul gave careful explanations of justification by faith, the meaning of the death of Christ, the process of sanctification, and spiritual gifts.

"For the wages of sin is death
but the gift of God is eternal life in Christ Jesus our Lord."

Romans 6.23, NKJV

BACKGROUND

Because Rome was the seat of the empire, it had great influence on the areas it controlled as well as surrounding nations. Even though the new faith of Christ was not proclaimed in any official governmental capacity, its presence in Rome still meant its proponents had a great deal of influence in spreading the new faith.

OVERVIEW

Paul's letter opened in the standard manner for letters of his time by including the name of the sender, the sender's titles, the name of the recipient and a greeting. Paul also included a brief summary of the gospel of Christ in the letter's opening.

A bondservant was a slave, a position Paul took on voluntarily out of reverence for Christ.

Paul acknowledged both the human (born of the seed of David) and divine (declared to be the Son of God) natures of Christ.

To impart a spiritual gift did not mean to present or give the believers a gift. Rather, Paul was saying that he would like to use his gift to bless his readers.

Though God had called Paul to preach to the Gentiles, his ministry was not limited to a type of person but was directed to all people.

Paul's understanding of the depth to which God had forgiven him and given him salvation led to his eager and unashamed desire to share the good news.

God's plan to give salvation to humanity began with the Jews, who He then called to be a witness to the rest of the world.

The righteousness of God is a theme found throughout Romans.

The truth of God has been revealed. Those who are wicked have chosen to suppress what they know to be true. Increased wickedness is the consequence of this suppression. Such choice and the resulting wickedness will one day be judged. Those who choose not to acknowledge God do not do so out of ignorance. God's characteristics are evident both in humanity and in all of creation. The need for God is so strong that those who refuse to acknowledge God create idols to take His place.

God gave them over is one indication of how God's wrath is at work. He allows those who reject Him to fall deeper and deeper into sin. In so doing they suffer greater and greater consequences and portray how completely depraved wicked people can become.

Paul clearly stated that sexual relations between two women or two men were *against nature* and not how God intended sex to be practiced and enjoyed.

Paul includes one of the most comprehensive lists of sins found in all of scripture. Sin is both a choice and a judgment. The consequences of sin form a part of the judgment those who choose sin will experience. At the same time, those who willfully reject God fall deeper into sin, encourage sin in others and experience ever greater judgment.

INSIGHTS

It is human nature to rationalize and rank sin. We tend to think, "This sin is not as bad as that sin," or "I may have done this, but at least I did not do *that*." Such rationalization and ranking can make us feel better and less guilty about our choices, but they do nothing to change God's view of sin or alleviate the judgment that results from continual and willful rejection of God and His ways. Though as sinful humans we cannot completely eliminate sin, we will go a long way by choosing to be obedient to God's ways rather than reject Him.

1. Paul longed to see the Christ followers in Rome so that they might *mutually encourage one another in each other's faith.* Why is it so important? Do you have someone in your life that fulfills this role for you? If not, who might God be calling you to enter into deeper Christian fellowship with?

2. Paul discusses a multitude of sins committed by man. Does he differentiate between types of sin, for example *gossip* vs. *murder*? Do you? Does God?

Romans, Chapter 2

BACKGROUND

Both Jesus and Paul talked about storing up treasures in heaven. Jesus advised people to focus more on treasures that would last into eternity rather than earthly treasures that would eventually perish (Matt. 6.20). Paul stated that doing those things that were displeasing to God was equivalent to laying up or storing treasures in heaven. These treasures would not bring the eternal benefit Jesus desired people to seek. Rather they were akin to storing up God's wrath, wrath that was not immediately realized but would be in the Day of Judgment.

OVERVIEW

This chapter focuses on God's judgment. His judgment is just, given according to one's deeds and based on what one knows. No one is exempt. God's judgment applies as equally to His chosen people as to those who hear His truth later.

In laying out his argument, Paul addressed an imaginary opponent, *you*, who embodied all that was wrong in approaching God. This was a common literary device of the time that was meant to teach rather than serve as a verbal attack.

Paul argued that those who were deep in sin could not adequately judge sin in others. Their judgment would always be tainted by a need to rationalize their own sin. Engaging in sin while judging those who also practiced sin did not make one righteous or divert God's judgment. God's judgment would prevail.

Eternal life is used to designate two different things, depending on the context in which it is used. When used to mean a current possession, it refers to the gift of salvation received by faith. When used of believers in the future tense, it refers to the eternal rewards God will give believers based on good work done on earth.

The Jew first did not mean that the Jewish people were more righteous or more deserving of God's judgment or grace. Rather, God's ultimate plan for salvation always included both Jews and Gentiles. God formed the Jewish nation to be a witness to the rest of humanity so that all people could realize the blessings of His grace.

Hearing the law was not enough to be saved by it. Only keeping (doing) the law would permit one to be saved. However, no one was/is able to keep the law to such a degree that salvation through it is possible. Paul later pointed out that the only means of salvation is through faith in Jesus Christ (3.24-26).

Those who do not know the Law of Moses have an innate sense of right and wrong implanted in their conscience by God.

When the Day of Judgment comes, people will be judged not only on what they did but also on their secret thoughts and motives as well.

Paul addressed the hypocrisy he saw in many of the Jewish people. They had been called as God's people and saw themselves in a superior role as guides, lights, instructors and teachers but would themselves engage in the things they instructed the Gentiles not to do.

Circumcision was not merely a physical and superficial ritual to be checked off when completed. Rather it was symbolic of a heart attitude that was obedient to God. It was therefore possible that the physically uncircumcised would better fulfill the law of God and one day stand in judgment of those who relied upon circumcision in a superficial and ritualistic manner.

INSIGHTS

As humans it can be tempting to reduce matters of great importance (relationship to God, parenting, marriage) to simple tasks that are easily accomplished. Simply checking off tasks on a list, however, does not mean we have achieved what we desire. Such matters require a significant investment of our time, a willingness to take risks, an openness to walk through the "ugly" parts of life, and a desire to learn and grow from our own mistakes. The hard parts of life *are* hard. The rewards for fully engaging in the difficulties are often beyond what we can imagine and generally lead to greater fulfillment than we would experience on the easy path.

1. Paul states, "God's name is blasphemed among the Gentiles because of you." In today's world, it is common for people to classify Christians as judgmental and hypocrites. Why is this? Are you aware of your responsibility to represent God to the non-believer? What are some ways you can positively represent Christ in your everyday life?

2. What does Paul mean when he says "... circumcision is circumcision of the heart, by the Spirit, not by the written code"?

ROMANS, CHAPTER 3

BACKGROUND

One method of presenting an argument in ancient times was to present questions or comments as if posed by an imaginary opponent. This allowed the speaker or writer to address issues that were important to his position without waiting for actual interaction with the listening or reading audience.

OVERVIEW

Having stated that circumcision does not lead to salvation, Paul posed the logical question, "What purpose does circumcision then serve?" He stated that circumcision was a sign of the oracles (the entire Old Testament) of God, which was entrusted to the Jewish people. The truth of God's promises was not negated by the unbelief of some Jews. God will be faithful to bring to pass all He said would occur.

God's judgment is just. Those who suggested God's judgment was a sign of His unrighteous wrath misunderstood who God is. Some might try to argue that their sin brings glory to God and, therefore, they should not be called sinners. Such an argument was so absurd Paul didn't even try to refute it. Instead he left those who made such an argument to God's judgment.

Jews and Gentiles were both equally guilty of sin. Paul paraphrased a series of Old Testament scriptures to prove his point. Those referenced can be divided into two parts. The first (vs. 10-12) focuses on humanity's deficiency, while the second part (vs. 13-18) points to humanity's depravity. Paraphrases are based on Ps. 14.1-3; 5.9; 140.3; 10.7; Is. 59.7-8; Ps. 36.1.

All of humanity stands guilty before God. Even those who claimed to follow the law could not be saved by it. The purpose of the law was not to bring salvation to sinners but to show the need for salvation from sin.

The Law and the Prophets was a phrase that meant the entire Old Testament.

The righteousness of God in this context is the righteousness God grants believers rather than referring to God's own characteristic of righteousness. Any person who chose to place their faith in Christ could be the recipient of God's freely given righteousness.

Since the curse of sin has fallen upon humanity, no one is able to live up to God's standards and all have sinned.

God's law demands justice, yet in His mercy, God provided a way in which sinful humans could receive righteousness instead of judgment. God's free gift was made possible by the willingness of His Son to take upon Himself the penalty of sin for all of humanity.

Some boasted in the law and their ability to keep its stipulations. Paul stated that no one could boast in their own ability, only in the *law* of faith, which is the only means to receive salvation.

If God gave salvation only to the Jews, He would be the God of the Jews. Paul stated that this is not true; there is only one God who is God of all, Jew and Gentile. Therefore, His salvation is not limited to only the Jews but is available to everyone.

INSIGHTS

Paul argued that God's righteousness – our salvation – is available only through faith in the Christ. It is human nature to want to *do* something. Yet salvation cannot be earned. Once we have placed our faith in Christ, our good works according to God's will and direction will earn us a reward in heaven, but they can never earn us salvation. For many people, this is beyond imagination. Their deeply colored pasts seem to demand some sort of retributive work before God would ever be convinced to give them such a gift. Such is not the case. God waits, ready to impart salvation to *anyone* who simply places his/her faith in Christ.

1. Paul told his readers that Jesus was presented as a sacrifice of atonement. If atonement is the reconciliation of God to humankind through Jesus Christ, is this reconciliation available only to some people or to all? How are we covered by Jesus' atoning sacrifice?

2. Paul taught that man is justified by faith and that the law plays no part in this justification. What does this mean? What is the difference between justified by faith and justified by the law? How do we ensure we are seeking justification through faith and not through the law?

BACKGROUND

Abraham was considered the father of the Jewish people. He was the first person to be called God's friend (2 Chron. 20.7). Abraham's willingness to depart for lands unknown, display the greatest trust in God's promises and obey God even at the cost of losing his son made him a model forefather whom the Jewish people continually upheld with great respect (Gen. 11.27-25.11).

OVERVIEW

Paul turned to Abraham to provide proof that justification (salvation) was achieved through faith and not through any type of works.

Paul first pointed out that according to Scripture, Abraham was not justified based on what he did. Rather, it was based on his faith that all God promised would come to pass (Gen. 15.6). Abraham believed God when He made His promises, not after he had a chance to perform works in any manner.

By quoting both the passage from Genesis and the Psalm of David (32.1-2), Paul presented the two witnesses required by Jewish law.

Paul's second point concerning Abraham was that he was credited with righteousness while he was still uncircumcised. A significant amount of time passed between Abraham being called righteous before God and his circumcision (Gen. 15.6; 16.3-4, 16; 17.24-25). Circumcision came later as a sign of the covenant God made with

Abraham. God would hardly make a covenant with someone who was unrighteous before Him. Abraham, then, became the father of all who believe, not just of those who would be circumcised.

Abraham and those who came after him did not receive the promises of God because of their adherence to the Law but because of their faith.

Those who are of the law means those who look to the law for their righteousness. It does not mean the Jewish people.

Since the law defines what is sinful, without the law there can be no sin.

From these arguments, Paul concluded that Abraham had not received righteousness through what he had done but through God's grace. And because his righteousness did not require adherence to the law or performance of any ritual, Abraham became the father of all who believed.

God brought life to the *dead* bodies of Abraham and Sarah, who were both beyond childbearing years, allowing Abraham to be called the *father of many nations.*

Abraham did not have some vague hope that what God said would come to pass. Instead he had a confident assurance (certain faith) that God's promises would be fulfilled.

Abraham's faith was not recorded to serve as an interesting story but as a model for all who would follow him. Faith in Christ would bring all believers the same justification that faith in God had brought Abraham.

INSIGHTS

Just as God made promises to Abraham millennia ago, so He makes promises to us today. Many of those promises are found in the scriptures, and periodically God may make a promise to us personally. As we evaluate those promises, we would do well to look at our attitudes toward those promises. Do we have faith as strong as Abraham's? Or is our faith more of a vague hope that God will come through? God wants us to have the faith of Abraham. He will respond to our prayers to strengthen our hope into an unshakable faith in the God who never fails us and always keeps His promises.

1. Paul described Abraham's great faith. Even when faced with no hope, Abraham in hope believed. Is there anything in your life that you believe is *against all hope*? Do you believe God can and will work in your life as He worked in Abraham's? If you have lost hope, how can you renew your hope in God?

2. What are some of the disciplines we can develop to strengthen and increase our faith? How does studying God's word help us to deepen our faith?

ROMANS, CHAPTER 5

BACKGROUND

The Greek word translated as *condemnation* is used only three times in the New Testament and each time by Paul in the book of Romans (5.16, 18; 8.1). It was used in a legal context to refer to the penalty that results from being convicted of wrongdoing.

Chapter and verse references in the Bible were added well after the New Testament cannon was compiled. Periodically, there are chapter or verse breaks that are not well placed in relation to the context. Such is the case with the beginning of this chapter.

OVERVIEW

The *therefore* which starts this chapter means Paul is drawing a conclusion as a result of the argument he presented in the previous chapter.

Sinful and rebellious humanity has been at war with God as they try to assert their own will over God's. Reconciliation occurs when individuals place their faith in Christ and receive the gift of justification from God. At that point, the individual experiences peace with God.

Rejoice in hope means to boast in the expectation of God's glory.

Rejoicing is not reserved just for a future hope but can be experienced in the trials and tribulations faced in daily life. God uses tribulations to develop endurance and ultimately mold certain qualities and virtues in the believer. The believer's faith is strengthened, and s/he experiences even greater hope in God and His promises. This hope will not be left unfulfilled because the God of love has poured Himself through the Holy Spirit into the lives of all believers.

Having mentioned God's love, Paul referred to the death and resurrection of Christ to show the depth of the love God has for humanity. No one would die for someone they judged unworthy and humanity's sin made them (us) quite unworthy of a holy God. Yet God sent His Son to die for the very humans who rejected and continually rebelled against Him. He did not first require any repentance from humanity but sent Christ to die while humans were still enemies of God. Reconciliation with God allows all who believe to rejoice in God for making reconciliation possible.

Paul included a comparison between Adam and Christ that covers verses 12-21. The comparison is interrupted by a parenthetical remark contained in verses 13-17.

The *one man* is Adam, whose disobedience to God caused sin and its consequence, death, to enter the world. All people have inherited the sin nature from Adam.

Just as sin came through one man, so God's grace, given as a gift, was made available to all through one Man, Jesus Christ.

Adam brought condemnation through his one act of disobedience while Jesus gave the gift of justification through His obedience.

When the law was given, sin was formally defined and its magnitude became apparent. Yet, God, through His Son, allowed grace to exceed sin, allowing life to surpass death.

INSIGHTS

It is only natural for humans to want to experience the "easy life." We don't want things to be hard, painful, or difficult to endure. Yet Paul states that growth in our character comes from the perseverance we experience in the midst of trials. The result of which is greater hope in and stronger relationship with God. Complaints about our trials can be replaced with prayers that seek to understand why God allowed the circumstances to happen, what He wants us to gain from the experience and how we can cooperate with what He is doing to cause His plans to come to pass.

1. Paul reminded his readers that no one chooses to die for an unjust man, yet God, through Jesus' death and resurrection, did just that. What does knowing that Jesus died for you while you were still God's enemy do for your appreciation and understanding of God? How can you show your gratitude to God for such a supreme sacrifice on your behalf?

2. Why does Paul encourage us to rejoice in our sufferings? How can adversity in our lives pull us into deeper communion with God? Recall a time in your life when adversity improved your character and drew you into closer relationship with God. What did you learn? How was God faithful to you during that time?

Romans, Chapter 6

BACKGROUND

Eternal life is used forty-two times in the New Testament. It usually refers to the gift believers receive at the moment they place their trust in Christ (John 3.16, 6.40). In eleven instances, however, eternal life is used to refer to something to be attained (Luke 18.18-30; John 12.25; Gal. 6.8). Eternal life, then, is not limited to a static gift. It is an evolving and growing relationship with Christ that begins at the moment one places his/her trust in Christ.

OVERVIEW

Having established the grace and redemption that were made available through the death and resurrection of Christ, Paul turned to the effects sin has on the believer.

Since grace will always be more abundant than sin, some people in Paul's time suggested there was no reason to turn from sin. In fact, they argued more sin would mean experiencing more grace. Paul stated this was in no way a reason to continue sinning. By believing in the work of Christ on the cross, each believer shares in His death and resurrection. Baptism is symbolic of Jesus' death (going under the water) and resurrection (being raised out of the water). Since believers are united with Christ in His death, they share in His victory over sin. As a result each should live the new and victorious life they have been given rather than remain in the old and sinful life they once had.

Old man refers to the sin nature of a person before becoming a believer. That nature shared in Christ's crucifixion and a new nature, one that has dominion over sin, shares in His resurrection. This dominion means believers are no longer slaves or in bondage to sin.

Freed from sin means no longer being obligated in any way to sin. Being freed from sin, however, did not eliminate sin and the mortal body can still be subjected to it. Paul admonished his readers not to give in to (obey) the lusts of their bodies.

Present your members referred to the individual body parts, tongue, hands, etc. Believers were to refrain from any sin and present themselves entirely to God.

Paul asked two questions concerning whether believers were free to sin. The first (v. 1) focused on a greater display of grace being evident through more sin. The second (v. 15) focused on whether sin was permitted since believers no longer live under the law. In both cases, Paul emphatically answered, "No!" In expounding on the second question, Paul stated that everyone is a slave to someone or something. To whom one was a slave depended on what they believed and how they acted. One could choose to be a slave to sin, which would lead to death, or a slave to God's righteousness, which would lead to life. Living as slaves to sin leads to ever more sin. Living as slaves to righteousness leads to holiness.

Paul shifted his focus from the choice each person has to make to the fruit such a choice will produce. The fruit of sin is death, but a new fruit is available to those who choose to serve God. That fruit is righteousness and eternal life. While death is the result of (payment for) sin, God gives the gift of eternal life freely to those who choose Jesus Christ.

INSIGHTS

The choice to be a slave to sin or a slave to righteousness is one each of us must make. The things and people we value and the beliefs we have give evidence to the choice we have made. The good news is that a choice to be a slave to sin (leading to death) can be overturned by choosing God's righteousness (life) instead. God wants us to choose life (Deut. 30.19). Though the world would have us believe otherwise, the choice to be a slave to God's righteousness will allow us to experience a more fulfilled life now and enjoy eternal life with God.

1. What does it mean to be a *slave to righteousness* instead of a *slave to sin*? Why does being a slave to sin result in death and a slave to righteousness lead to eternal life?

2. Paul encouraged his readers not to allow sin to be a master over them. Are you controlled by a sin pattern in your life? How can you free yourself from this bondage?

BACKGROUND

You shall not covet is the last of the Ten Commandments (Deut. 5.21). It is the only commandment that moves beyond one's actions and addresses the attitudes of one's heart.

OVERVIEW

Paul used the analogy of a woman whose husband had died to further explain the law's relationship to a believer. A woman was free to marry another man if her husband had died, but she remained bound to him in marriage as long as he was alive. In a similar manner, people were bound to the law until they placed their faith in Christ. At that point the law, in effect, *died* leaving them free to *marry* grace. This meant they were no longer bound to the law but to grace.

Just as marriage bears fruit by producing children, so grace bears fruit by producing righteousness.

In the flesh in this context refers to the time prior to placing one's faith in Christ. Death to the law means life in the Spirit, who prompts believers away from sin and toward righteousness.

People do not sin by following the law. The law was established to define sin. Sin can exist without the law, but no one would know what it was, and no judgment could be made about what was right or wrong.

Paul used himself and his own experiences as an example. He thought the law would bring life but found it brought death instead.

The holiness of the law is not at issue. People's inability to keep the law is what creates sin, not the law itself.

Paul's attempts to keep the law (in and of itself considered good) pointed to his inability to do so and his continual return to sin. The spiritual law and carnal flesh were continually at odds with each other. As a result, Paul found himself in the position of doing what he didn't want to do and failing to do what he knew he should. Paul had the will to do that which he desired, but he failed to follow through with his performance.

Paul used *inward man* to represent his mind, which delighted far more in the law of God than his flesh did. Paul called himself a *wretched man* because he had been defeated by sin. But Paul was not without hope. God had given him and all believers a solution. The solution was effective only if the problem was understood – wanting to follow God's ways but allowing the flesh to draw one into sin.

INSIGHTS

Each of us faces the same dilemma Paul faced. We often have a sincere desire to walk in God's ways, yet find ourselves drawn into sin. Sometimes that sin occurs because of willful disobedience while other times it is only after the fact that we realize our actions did not measure up to God's standards. In either case, sin has occurred. Just as Paul was able to rejoice in the hope he had in Christ, so we can rejoice in the same thing. God has given us the Holy Spirit to enable us to resist the temptation to sin. We can learn to draw more and more on the power He gives us to resist sin and temptation.

1. Paul confessed to his readers his tremendous struggle with sin, noting that he did not do the good he intended but the evil he did not intend. Can you relate to this? What sins do you continue to struggle with? How can you gain the upper hand?

2. Paul spends a lot of time focusing on the law, sin and death. What is the relationship between these three? What does it mean that sin leads to death? How do we win the battle against sin? What is in store for those who battle well?

Romans, Chapter 8

BACKGROUND

Abba is an Aramaic word that means *father*. It is used three times in the New Testament: once by Jesus when He was praying to His Father (Mark 14.36) and twice by Paul (Rom. 8.15; Gal. 4.6). All three times, the Aramaic word is followed by the translated Greek word.

In Roman times, children who were adopted into a family were entitled to the full rights of a biological child.

OVERVIEW

In the previous chapter Paul focused on what *living in the flesh* meant. In this chapter he turns his focus to *living in the Spirit*. Because believers no longer live under the law, the law cannot condemn them. Any condemnation one might have felt dissipates upon becoming a believer because all past sins are forgiven.

The Holy Spirit given through faith in Christ empowers believers to live in the righteousness of God rather than under the condemnation of sin and death.

Christ fulfilled the law and gave believers the means of gaining righteousness, not through the law but by being in Christ and living according to the Holy Spirit.

The carnal mind is a mind governed by sin, and therefore, at odds with or an enemy of God.

Being *in the flesh* means being an unbeliever or a sinner. It is different from *walking in the flesh*, which occurs when a believer foolishly chooses sin over God. While those *in the flesh* cannot please God because they are His enemy, those *in the Spirit* can rely upon His power and strength to live in a manner pleasing to God.

In addition to the empowerment of the Spirit, believers are adopted into the family of God and become joint heirs with Christ to the kingdom of God. Adoption means believers not only share in the suffering of Christ, they also share in His glory, a glory so magnificent that any suffering endured now will pale in comparison.

All of creation waits in eager anticipation of the unveiling of the children of God.

The firstfruits of a harvest were given to God in anticipation of the balance of the harvest yet to come. The firstfruits of the Spirit are a gift given by God in anticipation of the further workings of the Spirit yet to come.

Hope is the expectant anticipation of a future event or reality yet to be realized.

Paul told his listeners that weakness and uncertainty are no reasons to become discouraged when prayer is required. The Holy Spirit intercedes on behalf of believers when they are unable to do so themselves.

In the lives of believers, God does not let anything go to waste. All things, good and bad, are used to achieve God's purposes in and through a believer's life.

God's predestination does not negate human free will. All humans attain salvation under God's saving grace only when they chose to acknowledge the Lordship of Jesus Christ. God does not force anyone to do what s/he has not chosen to do.

Paul listed a series of experiences (opposition, v. 31; accusation, v. 33; and condemnation, v.34) that, on the surface, might appear to be obstacles to continuing a relationship with God. However, he concludes that nothing has the power to cause such a separation. Believer's can have confidence in God's continuing love.

INSIGHTS

While we are no longer under the condemnation of the law when we become believers, it can sometimes be difficult to feel that our guilt has been lifted. God forgives us of all our past sins when we come to faith in Christ. Yet sometimes we fail to forgive ourselves, choosing instead to carry a self-imposed burden of guilt. In these instances, we must learn to forgive ourselves in the same way God has already forgiven us. When we repent of our sin, God no longer counts it against us. Since God no longer counts it against us, neither should we. If we do hold it against ourselves, we are, in effect, stating we are better than God.

1. Paul reminded his readers that those who placed their faith in Christ would not experience condemnation because of their sin. Why is this truth so life saving for believers? What does this teach us about God's forgiveness and the importance of forgiving ourselves?

2. Paul described a Spirit who helps us in our weakness and intercedes on our behalf when we are unable or do not know how to pray. Do you wait until you know exactly what to pray? Do you try to handle things yourself? Do you think some things are too small, too great, too complicated, or too hopeless to be presented to God in prayer?

Romans, Chapter 9

BACKGROUND

Abraham had two sons, Ishmael and Isaac. God's promise to make Abraham the father of a great nation was to come through the son Abraham had with Sarah, namely his second son, Isaac. It was only the descendants of Isaac who became the nation of Israel. God also blessed Ishmael in a manner similar to that which Isaac received; however, it was through Isaac's lineage that the promised Messiah would one day descend (Gen. 17.19-21).

OVERVIEW

Having established specific truths about God as they relate to all believers, Paul turned his attention to his own people, the Jews. They had excluded themselves from God through their unbelief, and that pained Paul so much he was willing to be separated from Christ if it would mean his people would be united with Christ.

Paul listed some of the privileges his people inherited as believers. They were God's called people with whom He established His covenants, law and promises.

Paul pointed to both Jacob (Israel) and Abraham to show that being a physical descendant did not automatically mean one participated in inheritance of God. The sons of Isaac were yet another example. The promise was not fulfilled through Esau, the older twin, but through Jacob, the younger twin.

Paul voices the seeming unrighteousness of God choosing one over the other without regard for the good or evil they would do during their lives. This question is the theme of this and the following two chapters. Instead of attempting to answer the question, Paul pointed to God's mercy and sovereignty as He Himself expressed it to Moses (Ex. 33.19). God's choice is not based on a how a person acts but on God's mercy and compassion toward that person. God gave Pharaoh over to what was already in the ruler's heart in order to show God's own power.

Paul poses the question of how people can respond to God. Just as a potter can mold clay as he desires, so God can mold us as He desires as we choose to pursue or not pursue righteousness. He may choose patience for those who reject Him while trials may be used to better mold those who choose Him.

Paul returned to the question of Jew vs. Gentile. God's sovereignty allows Him to call both. Paul quoted from several Old Testament passages to make his point (Hos. 2.23; 1.10; Is. 10.22-23; 1.9). The Jews failed to obtain righteousness when they tried to do so by their own strength (works) rather than rely on God and take Him at His word (faith).

INSIGHTS

Paul's willingness to separate himself from Christ in order for his people (the Jews) to enjoy salvation is akin to Christ's sacrificial death on the cross — the ultimate sacrifice. How many of us are willing to make a similar sacrifice so that those around us who do not know God's saving grace may one day experience the unconditional love, acceptance and mercy of the God of the Universe? How much are our hearts burdened for the lost, the hurting, the underprivileged, and the marginalized? To what extent are we willing to go to reflect God's love and mercy?

1. Paul expressed great sorrow for and anguish over his people – the people of Israel – because they refused to accept Jesus and the truth of the gospel Paul also suffered because of the rejection he experienced from the people he loved. Have you ever been rejected or ridiculed by someone you love because of your faith? What was your response? How do you continue to extend love and grace to them?

2. Can you, with Paul, wholeheartedly state that God is just? How do you respond to those who say they cannot believe in a God who is unfair and unjust? How do God's justice and mercy interact?

Romans, Chapter 10

BACKGROUND

The Old Testament in particular states that righteousness is an attribute of God (Ps. 119.137, 142; 145.17). Through the covenant God made with the Jewish people, He called them to display His righteousness on earth by loving Him and loving others. In order to do so, the people had to follow God's commands and live morally upright lives. The Jewish people failed to reflect God in this way and ultimately came under judgment. By placing their faith in His Son, God gave both the Jews and Gentiles a means for being declared righteous.

OVERVIEW

Having laid the groundwork at the end of the last chapter, Paul turned to individual responsibility in achieving righteousness. Humanity was and still is responsible for its own sin. Trying to blame God's sovereignty and election would prove erroneous and futile.

While the Jewish people's refusal to exercise faith in God had become a stumbling block for them in their relationship with God, Paul earnestly desired and prayed that they would experience salvation. There was little doubt they were zealous for God, but their zeal was misplaced. *The end of the law* meant Jesus had fulfilled it and it was no longer required. Righteousness is achieved through Him.

Righteousness may seem difficult to obtain (as ascending to heaven or descending to the dead), but God's Word is much nearer than imagined: in the hearts and mouths of Paul's readers. Righteousness was and is obtained by confessing Christ with one's mouth and believing with one's heart.

Paul expounded on two approaches to righteousness. The first relied on keeping the law in its entirety. He had already established that this was not possible (Rom. 1-3). The second came through confession of Jesus Christ.

God will not reject anyone who calls on His Son. His righteousness is available to Jew and Gentile (Greek) equally.

Confession of Christ and His message of good news can only come through hearing that message, which itself will only occur if someone preaches it. Paul quoted Isaiah (52.7) to draw attention to the honor accorded to those who preach the gospel message.

Israel had not obeyed all the law commanded and would only move to a place of obedience by hearing God's Word.

In Paul's time (as now) people grappled with whether those who had never heard the message of Christ could be saved. Paul's partial quote of Psalm 19 (v. 4) pointed to creation testifying enough about God to draw those who had not heard the message of Christ to God.

God's judgment would come on Israel, not in condemnation but to draw them back into relationship with Him (Deut. 32.21; Is. 65.1-2).

INSIGHTS

Unbelievers sometimes justify their reason for not placing their faith in Christ by pointing to the debate about what happens to people who have not heard the message of Christ. God, in His justice *and* mercy will deal righteously with those who have not heard. Those who have heard the message can never use how God ultimately deals with people who have not heard the message of Christ as an excuse. God does not and will not judge any of us in comparison to those around us. Instead, He will judge each of us based on how we personally respond to Him and to the salvation offered through His Son.

1. Paul told his reader they would be saved by confessing Jesus with their mouths and believing God raised Jesus from the dead. How are *confessing with your mouth* and *believing in your heart* different? Why are they both so important?

2. What role do believers have in sharing the gospel of Jesus Christ? What are we called to do, once we believe?

Romans, Chapter 11

BACKGROUND

Paul calls himself by various ethnic names in his writings: Jew (Acts 21.39), Israelite (Rom. 11.1) and Hebrew (Phil. 3.5). These names all referred to the same group of people, though their technical definitions vary slightly. Hebrew was a racial name. Israelite was a national name and Jew a religious name that designated the descendants of Judah.

OVERVIEW

Paul used himself as an example to show that God had not turned away from the Jewish people. He cited another example by turning to the time of Elijah and the remnant God preserved for Himself during one of the darkest times in Israel's history.

Even in the times when the nation of Israel fell the furthest from God, God always maintained a remnant as a symbol of hope and a means of turning the nation back to Himself.

It is not possible to be under grace and works at the same time; each one excludes the other.

Israel sought righteousness but did not find it because of their unbelief. Paul used two Old Testament quotes (Is. 29.10; Ps. 69.22-23) to show God's judgment as a result of Israel's indifference. Israel had not fallen so far that they were beyond hope. Their transgressions brought salvation to the Gentiles, which in turn brought salvation to themselves.

The natural branches, as well as the olive tree, represented Israel. The grafted branches and wild olive tree represented the Gentiles. The tree no longer contained as many of its own branches because of Israel's unbelief. However, Gentiles had been *grafted* into the tree as they took God at His Word and believed in Christ. For both the natural branches and the grafted branches, the root was the same – the covenantal blessings God promised to Israel.

Paul warned the Gentiles not to become prideful of their position in God's grace and kingdom. The Gentiles were recipients of God's grace just as much as Israel was.

Paul wanted his readers to understand the mystery he was explaining so that they would not try to explain it in their own terms and thus become wise in their own eyes.

All Israel did not mean every individual but the nation as a whole. Paul paraphrased Is. 59.20-21 to reiterate God's promise of bringing salvation to the world.

Israel became an enemy of the gospel when they rejected it. However, their rejection did not prevent God from keeping the promises He had made to the patriarchs. God will have mercy on disobedient Israel and disobedient Gentiles.

Paul closed this section of his letter with a doxology, which acknowledged that God's wisdom is far beyond human understanding. He also recognized God as the creator, sustainer and focus of all things.

INSIGHTS

Though Messianic Jews have placed their faith in the saving grace of Christ, Orthodox Jews still await the Messiah. Just as Paul warned his Gentile readers not to fall into prideful, arrogant superiority because they were under God's saving grace and many of the Jews were not, so we too must guard against that temptation. The Jewish nation is still God's chosen people. God's promises yet to be fulfilled will come to pass in His time. We can wait in eager anticipation to see how God will work, both in our lives as believers and in the lives of His chosen people.

1. What did Paul say about the people of Israel and God's relationship to them? Has God, then or ever, turned away from the nation of Israel because of their disbelief? Do you see God's hand on the nation of Israel in world events today?

2. Do you believe anyone is unworthy of God's mercy?

Romans, Chapter 12

BACKGROUND

Spiritual gifts appear in list form in three main references in the Bible: 1 Cor. 12; Rom. 12.6-8; Eph. 4.11. The three lists overlap one another, but each contains gifts not included in the other lists. None of the lists are complete, though each list serves to encourage believers to use their gifts for the edification and service of the body of Christ.

OVERVIEW

Having completed the doctrinal part of his letter, Paul turned to practical instructions for living out one's faith. The first two verses of this chapter lay out the basic responsibility each Christian has in response to what God has done.

One's body being a living sacrifice meant it was to be used in service to God. Paul used three qualifiers to describe this living sacrifice. *Holy* means set apart for God's use. *Acceptable* means pleasing to God. *Reasonable* means an appropriate response to all God has done.

Spiritual transformation begins when people place their faith in Christ and continues throughout their lifetime. Paul commanded his readers not to be influenced or molded by the values of the world but to allow God's Spirit to transform their minds in order that they might more perfectly fulfill God's will.

Though the human body has many parts, all work together so the human being can function. In the same way, each new believer is given at least one spiritual gift for the benefit of the body of Christ. Though believers have different gifts and varying gift combinations, the use of all believers' gifts in the service of the body of Christ allows that body to function as God intended.

Love was not merely an emotion but showed itself in action, of which Paul listed several examples. The progression from helping fellow believers (saints) in need to showing hospitality is worth noting. Hospitality in Paul's time was particularly directed to housing strangers. As one helped fellow believers, opportunities would arise to help strangers and in the process show and share the love of Christ.

Blessing someone meant to speak well of him or her.

Be of the same mind meant to maintain harmony.

Paul's command to live *peaceably* with all people was limited to what the reader personally could do to cause this to come to pass. S/he was not responsible for how others acted but was responsible for his/her own actions.

Paul reminded his readers that God alone had claimed the right to take vengeance on another (Deut. 32.35). Those who had been wronged were to wait on God for retribution. This freed believers to show God's love to their enemies.

INSIGHTS

Today it can be tempting to limit our involvement in the body of Christ to attending church on Sundays. Yet, as Paul states, God has called us to serve one another and as we do so to reach out to nonbelievers. Each of us has been given at least one gift. We can begin the process of determining which gift(s) we have by taking a spiritual assessment or asking a trusted Christian friend or mentor. Gifts are not limited to one area of service. For instance the gift of teaching could be used for adult Bible studies, kids programs, or senior care. By combining our gift(s) with areas we are passionate about, we will discover the deep fulfillment of serving God.

1. As a member of the Christian community, how do you feel you can best serve? What are the unique gifts and strengths God has given you for the benefit of the church and others? If you are currently serving, are you utilizing your gifts? Is God calling you to take a risk for Him and use your gifts in a different context?

2. Paul provides a profound and practical set of instructions for living out one's faith. As you read these, in which areas are you doing well? Which areas need more attention? How might God be giving you wisdom and the tools to address the areas that need attention?

Romans, Chapter 13

BACKGROUND

The Pharisees tried to trap Jesus by asking whether taxes should be paid to Caesar or not. Jesus' answer to pay to Caesar the things that are Caesar's and to God the things that are God's not only sidestepped the trap but also affirmed government as a God ordained institution (Matt. 22.14-22).

OVERVIEW

Rulers and governments were established by God for the purposes of combating evil and promoting good. Because they are God-ordained, they are to be obeyed. This does not mean everything a ruler or government does is righteous, yet unless clearly against God's Word, the governing powers are to be obeyed.

Here the judgment may not refer to God's final judgment but to the judgment that comes through the God-appointed human authorities.

A believer's conscience was (is) affected not only by his/her civic duty to obey laws but also his/her spiritual duty to God.

Whatever was due to the existing government, whether taxes, respect, honor, etc., was to be paid.

Paul admonished his readers to pay anything owed to anyone, except for the one debt that can never be fully paid – loving one another.

Of the Ten Commandments, Paul listed four that were offenses against other people. He summarized these laws in the same way Jesus did (Mark 12.31). Loving one's neighbors fulfills the entire law.

Paul used *night* in a figurative sense to mean the current age in which Satan reigned and *day* to mean the coming of Christ when He would reign in glory.

The Greeks had wild parties that lasted well into the night and often included drunkenness and indiscriminate sex. Paul used this imagery to call his readers to cast aside all that belonged to Satan and put on the light, the goodness of Christ.

INSIGHTS

When the ruling authorities don't do what we believe to be right, it is often tempting to disobey the rules and laws. Yet God has called us to submit to the ruling authorities. Certainly there are times when disobedience may be warranted, such as in relation to the laws permitting abortion. The vast majority of laws, however, do not encroach on God's commandments and should be obeyed. There is nothing in scripture that prohibits believers from being involved in politics and working toward establishing laws that honor God and respect human life and amending or rescinding laws that do not.

1. What does Paul tell his readers about their interaction with authority? How do you manage your relationships with the authority figures in your life?

2. The command to love your neighbor as yourself can be found in the Old Testament, stated by Jesus in the Gospels and here, in Paul's letters. Why is love so important? How does love perfectly reflect God's character? How can you show God's love more fully to those around you?

ROMANS, CHAPTER 14

BACKGROUND

Jews generally believed that eating meat sold in the market place that might have been offered to idols was sinful. As a result, they often refused to eat any meat of unknown origin. Gentiles, with their pagan backgrounds, did not have a problem with eating such meat. In the same vein, Jewish believers wanted to continue observing the Jewish holidays that had little or no meaning to Gentile believers.

OVERVIEW

Paul designated as weak those who were bothered when they ate meat of unknown origin and described as strong those who could eat such meat without feeling guilty. Paul warned the strong not to despise the weak and the weak not to judge the strong. God was the master of all believers, and He was (is!) the only one who could rightly judge the righteousness or sinfulness of one's actions.

None of us refers to believers rather than people in general. Believers belong to God and, therefore, should do what is pleasing to Him. Ultimately, the issue was not the food or the day but whether what was done was being committed to the Lord.

All believers would one day stand before God and be accountable for their actions and decisions. Paul counseled his readers not to judge each other so they would not have to explain the division that existed between themselves when they stood before God.

Unclean was used to refer to things prohibited by Jewish ceremonial law.

Consideration needed to be balanced against conviction. Conviction that caused another to sin was too strongly held. By weighing conviction against consideration for the well-being of the other, a good balance would be achieved.

God's kingdom is not evident in external practices like eating and drinking but in internal qualities like righteousness, peace and joy. Putting service to Christ ahead of external practices would result in doing what is righteous before God and beneficial for fellow humans.

Paul exhorted his readers to pursue those things that would build up fellow believers, rather than cause them to stumble. God's work in them was at risk of being destroyed anytime a believer put his personal convictions above the work of God. Paul was not suggesting that such practices had to be given up entirely. Rather the believer should have faith that God permits such practices and honors those who refrain from them when around those who might stumble as a result.

INSIGHTS

Paul told his readers that God's kingdom was not evident in the external rituals but in the internal virtues. The same is true today. Rarely is anyone attracted to the Christian faith by the rituals that are observed. Rather they are attracted by the virtues that are displayed. Many people desire to feel peace, security, fulfillment and purpose. The ability to display such virtues in the midst of trials, suffering, and difficulties comes only through a conviction that God is who He says He is and will work in believers' lives for good beyond our own abilities. We can point others to hope by living out these and other virtues as God designed.

1. What does Paul teach us about judging others and accepting those who are different from us? Why is it important that we, as Christians, not judge one another? Who, ultimately, is the judge?

2. Paul warned his readers not to destroy the work of God because of food. What doe he mean? In your own life, is there anything that you might replace the word food with such as politics, worship music, outward appearance, etc.? Are you allowing a judgmental nature to undermine the work of God as you relate to others?

Romans, Chapter 15

BACKGROUND

Illyricum was a Roman province located north of Macedonia, along the Adriatic Sea and bordering Italy on the west. It is located in the general area of modern day Albania, Montenegro, Bosnia and Herzegovina, Croatia, Slovenia and southern Austria.

Whether Paul was ever able to journey to Spain is unknown. He did get his opportunity to minister to the Roman believers but not in the way he envisioned when he wrote his letter. He made the journey as a prisoner and had the opportunity to testify before the court (Acts 27-28).

OVERVIEW

Continuing on his theme of the strong being considerate of the positions of those who are weak, Paul suggested that the strong not do what would be personally pleasing to themselves. Rather, they should seek to do for the weak what is right and leads to their betterment.

Paul pointed to Jesus as the ultimate example of setting aside personal gratification in order that the weak (all of humanity) might be served.

Paul prayed that through scripture and in God, all believers might find unity with one another. Division among believers that resulted from a non-essential or a moral issue would not bring glory to God.

Paul concluded his discourse begun in 14.1 regarding strong and weak believers by calling all to unity in Christ to glorify God.

Christ came as the Messiah for two reasons: to fulfill God's promises to the Jewish forefathers and so that the Gentiles would see God's mercy and glorify Him. Paul quoted four Old Testament verses to show that God had always intended for the Gentiles to glorify Him (2 Sam. 22.50/ Ps. 18.49; Deut. 32.43; Ps. 117.1; Is. 11.10). The verses come from the three sections of the Old Testament, Law, Prophets and Wisdom, as well as three of the highly esteemed Jewish leaders, Moses, David, and Isaiah.

Paul had high regard for the Roman believers' goodness, knowledge and ability to hold each other accountable to the faith. Yet he also recognized they needed a reminder about some points of the faith.

Paul had been called by God to minister to the Gentiles as evident in the signs and wonders he was able to perform though the power of the Holy Spirit. As a result, Paul was able to glory in God as the Gentiles came to faith.

Paul quoted from Isaiah 52.15 to make his point that he wanted to continue taking the gospel to those who had not yet heard its good news. He planned to go to Spain via Rome. This would allow him to spend some time ministering to the Roman believers as well as being ministered to by them. Paul also hoped to be supported by them on his trip to Spain.

Paul hoped to visit Rome after delivering the contributions he had collected from Gentile believers to the Jewish believers in Jerusalem, a donation that would serve to bring greater unity to the Jewish and Gentile believers.

Paul requested prayers on his behalf for safety among the unbelievers in Judea (he had been warned of impending danger, Acts 20.22-23), successful results from his trip to Jerusalem, and the opportunity to journey to Rome as he desired.

INSIGHTS

Just as the Roman believers needed periodic reminders about certain aspects of their faith, so we, too, can benefit from similar reminders. It is often easy to forget God's promises in times of trial and temptation. At those times, reminders of who God is, what He has promised, and what He has in store for all who place their faith in Christ can serve to give us strength, perseverance, and hope. Such reminders come from reading God's Word, seeking the counsel of mature believers, praise and worship songs, sermons and fellowship with other believers.

1. Paul urged his readers to accept one another and live in unity with one another. Why is this important? What can happen to a church, a business, or a family, when unity fails and there is no longer a common goal to strive toward? How does unity bring glory to God?

2. Paul hoped his readers would be filled with joy and peace to the point of overflowing with hope. Is your life filled with joy and peace? If not, why not? Is God calling you to trust Him more so that He can fill you with more joy and peace?

Romans, Chapter 16

BACKGROUND

Kiss is used five times in the New Testament to refer to the sign of love and unity given among believers (Rom.16.16; 1Cor. 16.20; 2 Cor. 13.12; 1 Thess. 5.26; 1 Pet. 5.14). Four of the five times it is described as a *holy kiss*. This remained a common practice among church members for several centuries. Later abuses, however, caused it to be practiced only between same gender parties.

OVERVIEW

In the final section of his letter, Paul sent greetings to more than two dozen people. Though Paul had spent much of his letter discussing various doctrines and their applications, his extensive greetings point to what the doctrine was really about: loving, caring for and fellowship among people. Varying amounts of information are known about these people[4]:

- Phoebe – servant is used elsewhere to mean *deacon*; helper means *patron*. Phoebe was likely well off and provided her house as a meeting place for the local church.

- Priscilla and Aquila – always mentioned together, worked with Paul in Corinth and Ephesus (Acts 18); likely risked their lives in Ephesus; had a body of believers who met in their home.

- Epaenetus – a common slave name, though not exclusively; nothing more is known.

---

[4] Earl Radmacher, Ronald B. Allen, and H. Wayne House, editors, *Nelson's New Illustrated Bible Commentary* (Nashville: Thomas Nelson Publishers), 1454-1455

- Mary – one of six women in the New Testament bearing this name; nothing more is known.

- Andronicus and Junia – likely husband and wife as well as well known to the apostles.

- Amplias, Urbanus, Stachys, Apelles – all common slave names; nothing more is known.

- Aristobulus – potentially Herod the Great's grandson, though may easily refer to a different family.

- Herodion –*my countryman*; likely means he was of Jewish descent like Paul.

- Narcissus – thought to be a freedman and one of the empire's most powerful people under Claudius.

- Tryphena and Tryphosa – names come from a common root suggesting they may have been twins.

- Persis – nothing is known.

- Rufus – potentially the same Rufus as mentioned in Mark 15.21.

- Asyncritus, Phlegon, Hermas, Patrobas, Hermes – likely a part of a community of believers, all men.

- Philologus and Julia – may have been husband and wife; both names appear in other ancient documents in association with the imperial household of Rome.

- Nereus and Olympas – likely in a community of faith with the above people.

Paul warned against closely associating with those who were focused on causing division and offenses within the church. Such people were self-focused and had the potential to lead the church into permanent division if unity could not be maintained. The Roman church had been obedient, so Paul's warning was directed toward future caution rather than past offenses.

Except for Timothy, little is known of Paul's co-workers. Jason was Paul's host on his first trip to Thessalonica (Acts 17.5-9). Sosipater is thought to be the same person who accompanied Paul to Asia (Acts 20.4).

Paul spoke of salvation as a mystery because God's plan was initially hidden, then revealed in Jesus Christ.

INSIGHTS

The divisions that Paul warned against eventually took root in the church as is evident today in the many existing denominations. What has not changed, however, is that God sent His Son to die for the sins of all humanity that those people who chose to believe in Him might experience eternal life. Jesus sent the Holy Spirit that people might be empowered to spread His good news to the ends of the earth so that more people would have the opportunity to choose eternal life. And the Holy Spirit empowers each of us to love people that they might be drawn into the kingdom of God.

1. Paul warned his readers to watch out for those who cause divisions. What kind of damage can result from division? How could you guard against causing division or joining with those who would cause division? How can you encourage others to live united in Christ?

2. What scripture passage from Paul's letter to the Roman Church has impacted you the most? Why?

PRISON EPISTLES

The *Prison Epistles* refers to the letters Paul wrote the first time he was under house arrest in Rome. The four that make up this group of epistles are Ephesians, Philippians, Colossians and Philemon. Evidence within the books themselves suggests that they may have been written and delivered at the same time. For instance:

- Tychicus delivered the letters to both the Ephesians and Colossians, as well as news of how Paul was faring (Eph. 6.21; Col. 4.7-9).

- Paul mentioned his imprisonment several times in his letter to the Philippians (1.7, 12-18; 2.23). He also mentioned Caesar's household, indicating Rome was the place of his imprisonment (4.22).

- Onesimus journeyed with Tychicus to Colossae and then continued on to deliver the letter to Philemon (Col. 4.9; Phile. 10-17).

- All the letters are dated to the same period of 60-62 A.D.

EPHESIANS

Unlike some of Paul's other letters to the early churches, the letter to the church in Ephesus was not motivated by strife or contention among the believers. Instead, Paul focused on the person and deity of Jesus Christ. He told the Ephesian believers why Christ came, what He had accomplished and how that spiritual reality should impact the believers and their lives in the newly forming body of Christ.

The overarching theme of the letter is the unity believers in Christ should practice. Paul's ministry to the Gentiles brought Jewish and Gentile believers into the faith and body of Christ. As these previously opposing peoples came together in a united church, they also had the opportunity to unite against evil.

Ephesians can be divided into two parts. The first part, chapters 1-3, focuses on central doctrines of the faith found in Jesus Christ. The second part, chapters 4-6, discusses how a believer's life should reflect the truth of these doctrines.

EPHESIANS, CHAPTER 1

BACKGROUND

In ancient times, a small clay cylinder was used to impress an image in wax to seal a document in a container. The seal verified who sent the document and guaranteed it remained untouched as long as the seal was unbroken.

Jews during the time of Paul believed the end times could be divided into two periods: the time in which they lived and the time when the Messiah would come.

OVERVIEW

Paul's letter begins in a customary manner for ancient letters by identifying himself first, then the recipient, and finally offering a blessing. Some early manuscripts do not include the words *in Ephesus*. It is thought that the letter may have been written as a circular letter to the churches around Ephesus. *In Ephesus* may have been added at a later date to identify it among other letters Paul had written.

Paul began the substance of his letter by writing praises to God for the salvation that He offers all people through the blood of His Son (vs. 3-11).

The Jews believed God had *predestined* or chosen them through the covenant He established with Abraham. Paul, however, stated that one became a part of God's covenantal people through Christ rather than by their background.

Redemption means to "buy back" or "ransom." People sold into slavery to pay a debt could be *bought back* by paying the debt. Paul used the term here to indicate that Christ's blood paid the required debt to release believers from their bondage to sin.

The mystery of God was not something that was hidden or revealed only to certain individuals as in other religions. Rather it was His purpose that was hidden for a time but had been revealed to all through Christ.

At the appointed time, a time that only God knows, all things in heaven and on earth will be brought under the authority of Christ.

The Holy Spirit, given to all believers at the time they place their faith in Christ, serves as a seal of the promises of God and a guarantee that those promises, the inheritance of believers, will come to pass.

Paul prayed that the believers in Ephesus would know the hope of God's calling, the riches of His inheritance and His incomparably great power.

One demonstration of God's power was the resurrection of Christ, who was not only brought back to life but also placed in a position of honor and authority. Christ's authority would extend to those who chose to be His enemies (*under His feet*) and those who were inheritors of the kingdom (*head over all things*).

The church refers to all believers in the entire body of Christ rather than to a specific assembly of people.

INSIGHTS

Just as God blessed the believers in Paul's time with *every spiritual blessing*, so we too are blessed. In the trials, difficulties and mundaneness of life, it can be easy to lose sight of these blessings, yet they are with us whether we recognize them or not. The phrase *count your blessings* is often tossed around lightly but can be a good exercise in moments of despair and frustration. Giving serious thought to the ways in which we are blessed when we feel overwhelmed and out of control can serve to turn our focus from our frustrations to the provision and providence of God. In addition, counting our blessings in good times can keep us from foolishness that may cause life to fall apart.

1. Paul states that believers were chosen to be a part of His family before the world was every created. How does this truth impact your relationship with God?

2. How does the Holy Spirit serve as a guarantee of our inheritance in Christ? Why would God give us an *inheritance until redemption*?

EPHESIANS, CHAPTER 2

BACKGROUND

The ancient peoples, including the Jews, believed heaven had multiple layers (usually three or seven). Various beings or objects inhabited the different layers (angels, demons, stars, etc.). God and the purest of created beings inhabited the highest level of heaven.

The *middle wall* or *dividing wall* of the temple was the wall beyond which Gentiles were not permitted to pass. The penalty for a Gentile who passed beyond this wall was death. Paul had been falsely imprisoned on the charge of taking a Gentile past that wall.

OVERVIEW

The first part of this chapter contains one of the most comprehensive explanations of the gospel written by Paul in all of his letters. Not only did Paul address the issue that salvation came through faith in Christ by God's grace, he also stated that attempting to gain salvation through work of any type was not possible since salvation is a gift from God.

The believer's former walk was one made according to the ways of the world and the prince of the power of the air. *Air* was a term used to mean the atmospheric heaven (lowest level) where the evil spirits had dominion.

Lusts of our flesh referred to more than sexual desires. It included human desires for power, fame and wealth.

Dead in transgressions means spiritually dead. Adam's disobedience brought sin to the world and resulted in the penalty of both spiritual and physical death.

God made a new life free from the penalty of death possible because of His great love and mercy, and through the death and resurrection of His Son.

The means of attaining salvation is not through the work one does, which would allow one person to boast over another. Instead, God, in His grace, made salvation a gift that is freely given to anyone who believes in His Son. Faith, then, is the means of receiving salvation; it is not the cause of salvation. God's grace alone is the cause.

Paul was not suggesting that good works had no meaning; after all God created humans to do good works. Instead he was stating that humans should not trust in good works for their salvation.

Having stated the means by which individual Jews and Gentiles obtain salvation, Paul turned his attention to the new temple made of the united Jews and Gentiles on the cornerstone of Jesus and the foundation of the apostles and prophets.

God instituted circumcision as a sign of the Abrahamic covenant He made with His people. As a result, the Jews called themselves the *circumcision* and the Gentiles the *uncircumcision*.

The Gentiles had been without hope because they were not part of the Jewish nation. But God sent Jesus to the Gentiles as well as the Jews to give both hope and salvation.

God did not abolish the law but allowed what could not be fulfilled by humans to be fulfilled by Christ on behalf of all humanity. By so doing, God brought together two opposing peoples into *one new man* by the work on the cross so that all might have access to God through the Holy Spirit.

The apostles and prophets were the foundation because they pointed and testified to the work of Jesus. The cornerstone was the large first stone laid when a building was constructed. All other stones were lined up to the cornerstone. Because the Christian faith revolves around Jesus, He is the cornerstone of the faith.

INSIGHTS

Perhaps one of the best phrases in all of the scriptures is *but God*. After describing the old life of spiritual death that leads to physical death, Paul used the phrase to introduce the hope that comes from God. It is used repeatedly to introduce God's intervention into circumstances that seem hopeless or beyond the control of human beings. *But God meant it for good* (Gen. 50.20); *But God is the strength of my heart* (Ps. 73.26); *But God was with him* (Acts 7.9); *But God had mercy on him* (Phil. 2.27). God still intervenes today, and each of us can look to and for *but God* moments that give us life and fill us with hope.

1. What is the implication of Paul's statement that believers are saved by grace and as a gift from God and not by works? Are there ways you continue to try to earn your salvation? If there are, what can you do to confidently accept the gift of salvation God offers through grace?

2. Think back to the time when you were separated from Christ. What were the circumstances that brought you to place your faith in Christ? How is God calling you to have empathy for and speak into the lives of those who are separated from Christ?

Ephesians, Chapter 3

BACKGROUND

In Ephesians, Paul repeatedly used a somewhat insignificant phrase to mark a significant concept. The phrase *according to* (*kata* in Greek) pointed to God's blessings poured out on His people. These blessing do not merely come out of God's abundance but are in accordance with His abundance. In other words, God is not stingy with his blessings but gives lavishly in a manner that conforms to His abundance. (See Eph. 1.5, 7, 11, 19; 3.16, 20).

OVERVIEW

Verses 1-13 are a digression from the subject presented in the previous chapter. Digressions were a common part of Paul's writing style.

The subject of Paul's digression was God's revelation of the mystery of His grace that Jew and Gentile would be equals in His family. God's covenant with Abraham had stated that all the nations would be blessed through him (Gen. 12.3), but Paul received the new revelation that all people would be equals.

It was only through God's grace that Paul became a minister (servant) of His message.

Paul counted himself as least among the saints (the term Paul used to mean believers), yet had the privilege of preaching the richness of the good news of Christ to the Gentiles. Included in that good news was the mystery of equal fellowship among all believers, which God had kept hidden until He had revealed it to Paul.

God's mystery had not only been kept from humans in ages past but from angelic beings as well, who would learn about God's grace as it was revealed to humans.

Paul's prayer for the Ephesians included three items, none of which had to do with material goods, but rather centered on the growth and strengthening of the inner person. First, Paul desired that the Holy Spirit would strengthen them, which would allow Christ to dwell (take up permanent residence) in them. Second, through Christ's indwelling that they would know the magnitude of His incomprehensible love. Finally, that they would know the abundance of God's gifts in their lives.

Paul's closing doxology to this prayer pointed to God's power and love, which are both beyond and not limited by human imagination.

INSIGHTS

To Him who is able to do exceedingly abundantly above all that we ask or think is a testimony to the unfathomable ability of God. Often in our humanness, we fail to trust God. We may not pray because we believe God won't come through. We may not go as God commands because we think He is too weak to protect us. We may try to maintain control because we think we know better than God. In each case and many others, our beliefs and fears are based on a lack of trust that God is who He says He is. God can be trusted and taken at His word. He will do more than we can imagine if we are willing to walk with Him.

1. Paul marveled that he, the greatest of sinners, had been called by God to preach the message of grace to unbelievers. God has invited you into His family not only to love you but so that you can also help to advance God's kingdom. Do you have a sense of God's calling on your life? Are you fulfilling that purpose? If not, what step(s) do you need to take to follow God more closely?

2. Paul prayed a powerful prayer for the Ephesian believers. Is there someone you can pray a similar prayer over? Is there someone God is calling you to invest in so that they grow in the knowledge and understand of Christ?

EPHESIANS, CHAPTER 4

BACKGROUND

This time period of the early church marked a great change in God's plan of salvation with Gentiles being invited into God's kingdom on an equal basis with the Jews. Soon Christian Gentiles would vastly outnumber believers of Jewish heritage, thanks in large part to the Jewish apostles and disciples who made great sacrifices up to and including death. While the Jewish people were and are still critically important, the focus of the gospel turned to the *body of Christ* after Jesus' ascension.

OVERVIEW

For the remainder of this letter, Paul gave instructions to his readers about how to apply the doctrines he had written about in the first three chapters.

Paul referred to the Christian life as a walk. It was not a race to see who could finish fastest, or a test to remain stationary. Rather, it was constant and consistent progress toward the life each believer had been called to in Christ.

Paul suggested that the walk should be conducted with the same attitudes Jesus had displayed during His life on earth: lowliness (humbleness), gentleness and longsuffering (patience).

Faith in Christ places all believers in the same Spirit. Paul instructed his readers to endeavor (make every effort) to maintain that unity in Spirit. Just as there was (is) one Spirit, there was (is) also one body to whom all believers were called; one hope all believers would achieve; one Lord and faith in which all believers trusted; one baptism that sealed each believer's faith; and one God who reigned over all.

Baptism may refer to baptism in the Holy Spirit or water baptism. The latter was used to publicly identify a believer as a Christian.

Paul adapted the text of Psalm 68.18 to show Christ as the ascended Messiah who had triumphed over Satan and distributed gifts to His people.

Descended to the lower parts of the earth may also be translated as *descended to the lower parts, the earth,* meaning Christ descended to earth in the form of a man.

Paul listed some positions to which God calls various people to serve Him. These positions are referred to as spiritual gifts, with each believer receiving at least one at the time s/he received the gift of salvation. The purpose of the gifts was not for personal use or fulfillment but to prepare believers to go out and do the work of ministry so that the entire body of Christ might be built up.

Children are easily taken advantage of because they lack knowledge, wisdom and discernment. Paul encouraged his readers to use their gifts to bring all believers to a level of maturity in Christ so that they would recognize trickery and deceit and not fall victim to such practices.

Every person was essential to the full and proper development of the body of Christ as a whole.

Gentiles who engaged in immoral acts had their understanding so darkened they were alienated from God and could not see the truth. Paul encouraged Gentile believers not to return to such practices but to continue walking in the truth of Christ they had come to understand.

Paul spoke of *taking off* the old man and *putting on* the new man as one would take off filthy clothes and replace them with clean clothes. In so doing, Paul enjoined his readers to turn from sinful ways, replacing such practices with those that ministered to the body of Christ and were considerate of other believers.

INSIGHTS

Paul admonished his readers not to sin in their anger. When Jesus healed the man with the withered hand (Mark 3.1-5), He was angry with the Pharisees because they showed so little compassion and so much rigidity towards the law. Although Jesus had the legions of angels at His command, He did not retaliate or respond in any sinful manner. Likewise, there are instances when the anger we feel about a situation is righteous and warranted. In those instances especially, we must make sure our response is just as righteous and warranted and that we are not blindly striking out in retaliation and thereby sinning.

1. How do we walk in a manner worthy of Christ's calling on our lives? How do we live in lowliness, gentleness, patience and love for others when the world is encouraging us to live for ourselves, die with the most toys and get all we can without regard for others?

2. Paul contrasted the *old man* with the *new man* and called on his readers to be renewed in the spirit of their minds. What does this mean? How do we facilitate such renewal in ourselves? How do we encourage it in others?

Ephesians, Chapter 5

BACKGROUND

Sons of was a Hebrew way of stating a characteristic of a person. *Sons of disobedience* would mean that disobedience was a prominent feature of that person's character.

The Temple of Artemis (also called Diana), one of the seven wonders of the ancient world, was located in Ephesus. Artemis was the goddess of fertility and many pagan religious rituals were practiced in the city in an effort to appease the goddess and ensure continued fertility, both agriculturally and in humans.

OVERVIEW

When God initially communicated the requirements of the sacrificial system to Moses, some of the sacrifices were intended to be sweet aroma to the Lord (Ex. 29.18; Lev. 1.9; 17.6). The ultimate sweet aroma came from Jesus' sacrificial death on the cross, which was done out of deep love for humanity. Paul encouraged his readers to use Jesus as a model and extend sacrificial love to others.

Paul warned against the numerous immoral pagan practices that many of the new believers would have been familiar with and even participated in prior to their conversion. There was no place for fornication (sexual immorality), uncleanness and covetousness in the life of a Christian. In addition, Paul warned that people who engaged in such practices would not only be unable to inherit God's kingdom but they would also be subject to God's wrath.

Good and evil were commonly represented by light and dark. Paul used these terms to instruct believers that just as their position in the kingdom of God had changed, so should their walk.

The origin of Paul's quote is unknown. Some think it may have been an early Christian hymn. Whatever its origin, it was likely familiar to the early Christians.

Redeeming the time meant to make the most of the time or take advantage of the opportunities to serve.

Walking in the ways of the Lord required wisdom and was not based on how one felt.

Being filled with alcohol (wine) put one under its influence and resulted in immoral behavior and excessive personal pleasures. On the other hand, one could choose to be filled with the Holy Spirit. Under His influence, one's actions would be in line with the will of God.

The three types of songs Paul mentioned, psalms, hymns and spiritual songs, are often viewed as referring to the Psalms and psalm-like scriptures, songs addressed to God and songs about the Christian life. Thanksgiving is a natural result of the wisdom and understanding Paul encouraged his readers to cultivate.

The last part of this chapter and first four verses of the next address how members of the body of Christ should relate to one another.

The word translated as *submit* means to voluntarily accept the authority of another person. Christians were to submit one to another (v. 21), as were wives to their husbands (v. 22). In the context of the earlier part of the chapter, submitting to others would not include engaging in wrongdoing or questionable behavior. Each believer was first responsible to God and then to submitting to one another.

Paul's emphasis for husbands was on the sacrificial love they were to show their wives.

The union between Christ (as bridegroom) and the church (as

bride) is very similar to the union of man and wife in marriage and is the great mystery God revealed.

INSIGHTS

Authority exists within the Godhead. Jesus submitted to the authority of the Father (John 5.19), and the Holy Spirit came as Jesus promised to empower, comfort and help believers (John 15.26). Within the Godhead, however, the Father, Son and Spirit are equals. In a similar manner, God's design for marriage places the spouses in partnership as equals and at the same time places the wife under the authority of her husband. The husband is called on to extend to his wife the sacrificial love Jesus demonstrated when He willingly submitted to death on the cross. Though many in our society today would not agree, wives may well have the easier role!

1. How can we imitate and extend to others Christ's sacrificial love on a daily basis? Why is it easier to show such love to some people and harder to others?

2. How do we remain in the light of the God's truth and avoid becoming entangled in the darkness of lies, deceit and disobedience?

EPHESIANS, CHAPTER 6

BACKGROUND

Roman soldiers were instructed to stand their ground in the face of attack. They were not to retreat. Guerilla warfare was not practiced at this time and most battles took place on large open fields. As long as the soldiers maintained their formation and did not break ranks, they were very difficult to defeat. In telling the Ephesians, *Stand therefore* (6:14), Paul used this imagery as a metaphor for the spiritual battle believers were engaged in.

OVERVIEW

As Paul continued his dialogue on relational matters, he turned to the relationship between parent and child. Children were admonished to obey the commandment by honoring their parents. Paul did not put the entire onus of the relationship on the children, however. Parents were warned not to be too overbearing or severe with their children.

Paul voiced a very uncommon opinion when he suggested that slaves and masters were equals. Slaves and masters were to treat each other much the same way, serving each other fairly and righteously. Each was to be motivated by the knowledge that they were ultimately servants of Christ, who would treat all fairly regardless of their position on earth.

Paul warned his readers that they had to be on guard against the attempts of Satan to derail them from their Christian faith. While such battles can occur with other human beings, the majority of Satan's battle is waged through forces that cannot be seen.

Paul encouraged his readers to withstand so that they could stand. It is only by protecting oneself and engaging in the battle that one can hope to survive the spiritual war that does and will take place.

Paul mentioned six pieces of spiritual armor that believers can use to prepare for and engage in battle. Four of the pieces were named specifically while two (belt and shoes) were implied. All the pieces were used for defensive purposes except for the last, the sword of the Spirit. The word of God, which acts as the sword of the Spirit, refers to the specific word a believer might need in a given situation. Knowing the specific word comes through study and memorization of scripture passages. All the pieces of spiritual armor are obtainable by any believer.

Full armor would have no effect without prayer. Paul not only encouraged his readers to present their prayers to God but also to pray that he would continue to boldly present the gospel and serve as the ambassador for Christ, a position given to him by God.

The only mail system in Paul's day was reserved for imperial business. Travelers carried all other mail, hence Paul sent Tychicus to deliver his letter and let the believers of Ephesus know firsthand how Paul was faring under Roman house arrest.

INSIGHTS

Paul's warning to be on guard against the tricks of Satan is just as valid today as it was when he wrote the letter. Satan is still trying to use whatever means he can to either turn us from faith in Christ or make our faith ineffective. He may use subtle means that lead us away from a strong and vibrant faith in Christ. He may use catastrophic events to cause us to doubt God's goodness and His concern for us. He may tempt us in areas of weakness that lead us to a life of sin. Today we can put on the same armor of God available to the early Christians. Such armor is put on by knowing scriptural truth, living obediently and trusting Jesus. Reading scripture on a daily basis, even if only for a moment or two, is a great way to begin gaining scriptural knowledge and truth.

1. As parents, how can we balance training children in the ways of the Lord and not provoking them to anger?

2. How can we practically put on the various pieces of spiritual armor each day? How does intentionally preparing for spiritual battle make us better able to stand against the attacks of the enemy? Are there one or two pieces of spiritual armor that you need to don more regularly?

PHILIPPIANS

Paul wrote his epistle to the Philippians when he was imprisoned in Rome. This proves to be a significant fact because the main focus of this letter is joy. While happiness is based on circumstances, joy is the result of an inner peace that comes from God. Paul was able to find joy, especially joy in serving Jesus, even as he experienced the life of a prisoner.

It is thought that the hostility Paul experienced in Philippi during his second missionary trip (Acts 16.16-24) was directed toward the new believers after he left. Paul heard about their ongoing suffering and wrote this letter to encourage the relatively new believers in their faith. Though they experienced suffering, it was not in vain. Suffering endured as a result of faith in Christ and advancement of the gospel would one day be rewarded.

Paul also wanted to warn the believers about those who would take advantage of them rather than build them up in the name of Christ. False teachers abounded, and it required both knowledge and discernment to recognize and counter those who preached lies.

Philippians can be divided into four parts along chapter breaks. The first chapter gives an account of Paul's circumstances and focuses on what he had learned through them. The remaining chapters focus on the mind of Christ, the knowledge of Christ and the peace of Christ respectively.

PHILIPPIANS, CHAPTER 1

BACKGROUND

Paul used the word *joy* five times in this letter (1.4, 25; 2.2, 29; 4.1), and two related words translated as *rejoice, joy or glad* are found ten times (twice in 1.18; twice in 2.17; twice in 2.18; 2.28; 3.1; twice in 4.4).

Bishop referred to those who oversaw the spiritual well-being of the church. *Deacons* referred to those who dealt with the physical and material aspects of the church. The mention of both types of leadership at the church in Philippi suggests it had grown considerably.

OVERVIEW

Paul's first visit to Philippi took place during his second missionary trip (Acts 16.12-34).

In Paul's three other prison epistles (Ephesians, Colossians and Philemon), Paul introduced himself as an apostle. Here he used the word servant (bondservant) to describe both himself and Timothy.

Paul was filled with joy for the Philippians as he interceded on their behalf.

Paul was confident that God was and would continue to be at work among the Philippian believers until the return of Christ.

Paul used two legal terms, translated *defense* and *confirmation*, which may have implied he was looking forward to his upcoming trial or gave an indication that he continued to preach the gospel boldly while under house arrest. In either case, he counted the Philippian believers as his partners in his ministry. It is known that the Philippian church financially supported Paul, and this may have been the basis for the close partnership.

Paul's prayer that the believer's love would increase was based on two things. First was knowledge, which implies an established relationship that allows for direct and personal understanding. The second was discernment, which also revolves around understanding, this time on a moral or ethical level. Well-developed knowledge and discernment based on love would lead to greater purity and righteousness.

Paul reassured his readers that the spread of the gospel was not being hindered by his imprisonment. In fact, Paul was able to preach the good news to areas that would normally have been closed to him: the palace guard and the ruling house (4.22).

Paul took issue with the motive (not doctrine) from which some people preached. Their motive seemed to be based on a desire to aggravate Paul's imprisonment as much as possible. Paul rejoiced that the gospel was being preached and left the motive as an issue between the preacher and God.

Paul was supremely confident in God and His ability to work through Paul. Paul's deliverance would come no matter what happened. If he died he would be delivered to Christ. If he lived, he would have continued opportunity to spread the good news of the gospel. Paul's desire to be with Christ was equal to his desire to serve the needs of many believers as well as those yet to hear the gospel, leaving him uncertain as to which was more desirable.

At the end of this chapter, Paul gave the first of several commands to his readers. They were to focus on and act in ways that were worthy of the gospel. Part of doing so was being united within the body of Christ. The Christian faith was not meant to be lived in isolation but in fellowship with other believers. Their ability to stand against persecution would itself serve as a testimony to the good news of Christ.

INSIGHTS

Paul was so certain of his faith and the work of Christ that it did not matter to him whether he lived or died. Many believers today do not have that confidence. They desperately hang on to life or ardently fear death. Either position can lead to a compromise of the gospel. God wants each of us to have the same confidence Paul had. Such confidence can give us great freedom as we realize that both our life and death will honor God and will be used by Him to further His kingdom. It also gives us a greater boldness to speak God's truth because fear of the response is replaced by trust in God's sovereignty.

1. Are you as confident today as Paul was about his readers that God, having started a good work in you, will be faithful to finish what He has started in you? Do you fully cooperate with the good work God is doing in you?

2. Though his prison experience itself must have been very trying, Paul rejoiced in the event because he could see how God was using it to spread the gospel. During your times of trial and suffering, are you able to see how God is using you and your faith in Him to further the good news of Christ? If you have not been able to, can you pray that God would open your eyes to the work He is doing in you and through your hardship?

PHILIPPIANS, CHAPTER 2

BACKGROUND

Philippi was founded in the fourth century, B.C., and named after King Philip of Macedon. The thriving little city of Philippi still exists in northern Greece. Archaeological work in Philippi has revealed a large forum, a theater and allegedly, the jail in which Paul and Silas were held. The major road, known as the Egnatian Way, from Rome to Byzantium (modern Istanbul) ran through Philippi, allowing Paul to easily travel that area. Philippi is north of modern Thessaloniki, Greece, home of the Thessalonians to whom Paul also wrote.

OVERVIEW

The *therefore* that starts this chapter ties together the conflict Paul was experiencing with the conflict the Philippian believers were experiencing. In both cases the conflict could rule attitudes and destroy the unity that was to exist in the body of Christ. Paul had shown how he had risen above the conflict that surrounded him to continue proclaiming the truth of Christ and called the Philippians to do the same.

In his earlier statement, Paul was not condoning the selfish motives with which some preached the gospel. He clarifies that the proper attitude of all believers is selflessness and a concern for others that regards others higher than oneself and their interests equally with one's own.

Paul pointed to Christ as the example the Philippians should strive to be like. Jesus left his position of deity and took the lowly position of servant-man. He not only gave up all he was entitled to but also endured the worst imaginable death, all in humble obedience.

The Greek word translated *form* means the nature of Christ is the same as the form in which He appeared. In other words, being in the *form of God* means Christ is God while being in the *form of servant* (a human endeavoring to carry out the will of another) means He is a servant. The Greek word translated *likeness* does not mean similarity. Rather it points to identity. Christ is not like a man but is a man. Paul's statement that Christ was fully God and fully man is one of the most significant scriptural statements concerning Christ's incarnation.

Christ's humble obedience resulted in His exaltation to the very highest position in heaven. Not only does God elevate Him but He also is and will be honored by all of creation.

Paul encouraged the Philippians to *work out* their salvation. This implied a growing in the gift freely given to them by the completed work of Christ on the cross. Note that Paul did not tell his readers to work *for* their salvation.

Paul warned against dissension that could take root in the midst of the Philippian church. They were to be on guard against the negative cultural influences that surrounded them. To the world around them, they were to be a testimony of God's goodness, not let the world be a testimony to them.

Paul sent two ministry companions to the Philippian church. The first was his coworker, Timothy. The Philippian believers were familiar with Timothy and knew him to be a man of good character. The second was Epaphroditus, likely a member of the church at Philippi who had been sent by that body to bring gifts to Paul (4.18).

INSIGHTS

One of the mysteries of the Christian faith revolves around the nature of Christ; that He is both fully God and fully man. While the mechanics of how this could be possible will remain a mystery, what can be said is that Jesus' fully human nature allows us to identify with Him. He is not a distant God who has no involvement in human affairs. Rather, He can intimately identify with the human condition because He is human. At the same time, Jesus' fully God nature means He is completely worthy of our trust and worship.

1. Christianity is the only religion in which God became man. Why is it significant that Jesus left the throne of heaven and lived as a man on earth? What does it mean for our faith in Jesus that He submitted to the authority of His time, suffered, died and trusted in His Father for new life?

2. Paul called the Philippians to go about their lives without complaining or disputing. How can you incorporate this practice into your life today? How does incorporating such a practice necessitate ever-increasing trust in God?

PHILIPPIANS, CHAPTER 3

BACKGROUND

In ancient times, dogs were seen as scavengers. Jewish teachings stated that dogs were unclean and sometimes sexually immoral. Though dogs were used for guarding both houses and flocks, they were more often despised than loved as pets. The term came to be used for those who were morally impure or cruel and fierce enemies. The term is used numerous times in the scriptures to indicate reproach (1 Sam. 17.43; 2 Kings 8.13; Is. 56.10-11; Rev. 22.15).

OVERVIEW

Finally served as a transitional statement rather than a conclusion to the letter. Paul's previous statements all pointed to rejoicing in the Lord. God was in control, allowing Paul to rejoice even in prison.

Paul's main concern for the Philippian believers was that they did not fall into heresy. His warning against dogs, evil workers and mutilators was an exhortation to avoid the destructive doctrines taught by false teachers in their midst. *Mutilation (mutilators of the flesh)* referred to circumcision, which Judaizers insisted was necessary for salvation to occur.

Spiritual circumcision was a matter of the heart, not the flesh. Paul included three aspects of such circumcision: worshipping God in the Spirit, rejoicing in Christ, and placing no confidence in human accomplishment.

If anyone could have confidence in human accomplishment it was Paul. He was a Jew in every sense one could be, yet recognized that being a Jew was not enough to be righteous before God. Righteousness had to come from God, not from who a person is or what s/he does.

Everything, including those things Paul once highly valued, was now without value when compared to what he had received in Christ. Paul had attempted to gain righteousness through the law but he had since learned there was no value in that either. Only righteousness given by God through one's faith in Christ actually made one righteous.

Paul wanted to not only know the power of Christ's resurrection but to also share in His suffering as well. He placed obedience to God at the highest level and was willing to be obedient even in death, if that was required.

The Greek word translated *perfect* means mature, complete or finished, rather than sinlessness or flawless as modern day readers might interpret.

Paul used the analogy of running a race to describe his efforts to share in the suffering, death and resurrection of Christ. He *pressed on* to achieve the goal. The Greek form of the verb indicates this is a continuous action.

Paul called the Philippian believers to strive toward maturity and be open to any correction God might reveal to them.

The *enemies of the cross of Christ* were those people who focused on earthly things instead of the reward God gives through faith in Christ. *Belly* referred to the physical appetites (sexual or dietary) that consumed many people. Since the things they hoped in and took pride in would actually bring disgrace and shame, they were headed for destruction.

Believers are citizens of heaven who temporarily reside on earth. As a result, believers focus on and eagerly await the return of Christ, unlike nonbelievers who are focused on earthly things.

INSIGHTS

Immigrants often experience conflict between the way they were raised and the customs of their new home. Efforts to maintain their native culture as well as lack of understanding and judgment about cultural practices by the members of their new culture are just a few of the areas where conflict can arise. In many ways believers experience the same types of conflict. As God makes us new creations in Christ and we grow in our heavenly citizenship, we find conflict arises with the earthly culture in which we continue to live. Such conflict presents continued opportunities to trust in God's grace and sovereignty.

1. Paul once thought he could, if anyone could, have confidence in the flesh, i.e. in his own ability to be righteous and blameless before God. Is there anything other than faith in Christ that you put your confidence in in order to be righteous before God? How can you set aside misplaced confidences and have complete confidence in Christ to make you righteous and blameless before God?

2. It can be tempting to hold onto shame, bitterness, anger and other attitudes about our pasts. How can we, like Paul, move our focus from the past to the future? How can we continually press on toward the goal of God's call on us in Christ Jesus?

Philippians, Chapter 4

BACKGROUND

The Bible mentions a book, called the *Book of Life*, in which the names of believers are written. John, the author of Revelation, used the term most often and repeatedly referred to names being written in or blotted out of this book. Those who believe in Christ will find their names in the Book of Life and enjoy eternal salvation while those whose names are not found in the Book will be condemned to eternal death (Dan. 12.1; Ps. 69.28; Rev. 3.5; 13.8; 20.15; 21.27).

OVERVIEW

Paul called the believers in Philippi his *joy and crown*. They were the reward for his efforts of preaching the gospel in the region.

Little is known about Euodia and Syntyche, two women in the Philippian church. Paul *urged* rather than commanded them to be like-minded with Christ. This would seem to indicate there was some type of conflict or perhaps competition between the two that Paul thought would be solved by remembering and following the example of Christ. Paul continued to view them fondly as he reminds his readers they (along with Clement and others) labored for the sake of the gospel with Paul. The identity of Paul's *true companion* is unknown.

The joy believers experience is not based on the circumstances in which they may find themselves but in their relationship with God. As a result, they (we) can find joy in all things. Note, this is not joy because of the circumstances but in the midst of the circumstances.

Gentleness means consideration. Paul was encouraging the Philippian believers to put the needs of others ahead of their own.

Feeling anxious is a common response to trials and difficulties. Paul exhorted his readers to replace worry with prayer and trust that God would provide.

Guard was a military term that referred to preventing invasion by the enemy or preventing the enemy from escaping. God's peace would act in the same way over the heart and mind by protecting one from outside evil influences and helping to maintain an internal focus on God.

Paul commanded his readers to meditate on things that are:

- true – as found in God's Word
- noble – worthy of the King of the universe
- just – impartial, fair
- pure – sacred, holy
- lovely – beautiful, appealing
- of good report (admirable) – uplifting, charitable toward others

As Paul expressed his gratitude for the provisions the Philippian believers had supplied, he also revealed how deeply his trust in God had grown. He had learned to be content despite the circumstances because the strength he found in Christ provided all he needed.

Paul's reliance on Christ's strength did not mean he was not grateful for the gift the Philippians had sent. Just as important as the gift itself was the Philippians' willingness to give. It was a sign of spiritual maturity that Paul was equally glad to see. *Sweet-smelling aroma* and *acceptable sacrifice* indicate Paul viewed the gifts as much as an offering to God as they were gifts to him.

Just as God met Paul's needs through the generous giving of the Philippians, so the needs of the Philippians would be met through God's provision.

Caesar's household likely meant believers who were officials in the Roman government or servants in the royal household.

INSIGHTS

The world's constant and consistent message of *more, buy, whoever dies with the most toys wins*, etc. is in direct opposition to Paul's advice to be content in all things. The world's message leads to dissatisfaction, disappointment and disgruntlement. On the other hand, being content leads to peace, satisfaction and joy. In the face of keeping up with the Jones', contentment can be a hard virtue to cultivate. God desires us to be satisfied with what He has provided and trust in Him for future needs. In so doing, we create the opportunity to learn about and appreciate the deepest joys in life and God's best for us.

1. Paul encouraged the Philippian believers to bring all things to God in prayer. Do you do this? How can trusting God with everything we face – trials, suffering, worry, anxiety and hardship – lead to peace we cannot understand? Have you experienced such peace standing guard over your heart?

2. How can meditating on things that are true, noble, just, pure, lovely, of good report, virtuous and praiseworthy change your attitude toward life, even change your life itself? Why are these items so important to God's peace being with you?

COLOSSIANS

Paul's letter to the believers in Colossae was written in order to counter heresy that was creeping into the church. The specifics of the heresy are unknown, though it was likely a combination of legalistic Judaism and pagan beliefs that were prevalent at the time. In this erroneous teaching, Jesus was not viewed as the God-man who came to earth to offer salvation to all of humanity.

Paul's letter to the Colossians has particular relevance in today's culture. Many believe Jesus was a "great teacher," but was not God. Paul lays out a careful argument for the deity and supremacy of Christ and the need to keep Him central to the Christian faith and worship.

Colossians can be divided into two parts. The first two chapters focus on the sovereignty of Christ and the sufficiency of His atoning death and resurrection. The second two chapters focus on how the presence of Christ impacts the lives of believers.

Colossians, Chapter 1

BACKGROUND

Colossae was a prosperous city about 12 miles from Ephesus, with a main road connecting the two. The city received its name from the dark red wool called *colossinium* produced in the region. The trading wealth of Colossae attracted Jews, Greeks and Phrygians and their various philosophies, the errors of which Paul felt the need to address. Epaphras, Philemon and Philemon's slave, Onesimus, were citizens of Colossae. All that remains of Colossae today is a large hill that has not been excavated.

OVERVIEW

Just as he had with other bodies of believers to whom he had preached the gospel, Paul offered thanksgiving and prayed for the believers in Colossae (Eph. 1.16; Phil 1.4; 1 Thess. 1.2).

In several letters, Paul used the words *faith, hope* and *love* together as he does in the opening of this letter. The Colossian believers' faith was grounded in Christ, which caused genuine love to pour out to others and hope to find its ultimate fulfillment in heaven.

Epaphras is thought to have been one of Paul's converts and a fellow prisoner who was originally from Colossae.

Paul prayed that God would give four things to the Colossian believers: knowledge, wisdom, strength and joy.

Walk worthy of the Lord was to live in a manner that reflected what God had done and was doing in them.

The Colossians' strength was not to come from their own ability but from the power God gave His people. The result of such empowerment is patience (endurance) and longsuffering (restraint, even-temperedness) accompanied by a deep joy.

Qualified means authorized to perform. Believers cannot qualify on their own. Instead, they are qualified by God's grace through the work of Christ.

Light and darkness were common symbols for good and evil.

Paul's recitation of Christ's supremacy (vs. 15-20) is thought to be an early Christian hymn.

Firstborn did not necessarily mean the first child born. In Jewish culture, it often referred to the rightful heir. (Isaac, Jacob and David were not firstborns, yet each became heir to his father's line). Jesus is the firstborn over all creation and the first born from the dead because it is through Him that believers are able to experience the new life that comes from redemption and salvation.

That Christ will one day *reconcile all things* to Himself does not mean that all people will one day be saved. It means that creation, currently in an adversarial relationship with its Creator, will one day be brought into a peaceful relationship.

Christ does offer reconciliation to any who accept the salvation He offers. Those who believe will one day be presented to God as blameless and without reproach.

The gospel preached to *every creature under heaven* may be an exaggeration Paul used to explain the rapid spread of the gospel.

Lacking in the afflictions of Christ meant facing the suffering Christ would have endured had He still been in the world.

Paul used *mystery* to refer to a similar concept found in Eph. 3.8-10. God kept hidden certain aspects of His plan for salvation until Paul's time when He called Paul to reveal to the world that Gentile believers could receive salvation on an equal basis with Jewish believers.

INSIGHTS

The significance of Paul's statement in 1.21-22 should not be missed. The disobedience of Adam caused sin to enter the world. Living in a fallen world means that all people are born with a corrupted or sinful nature. The only hope for redemption comes through the death and resurrection of Jesus Christ. For all who choose to believe and receive the free gift of salvation, their sins are forgiven. One day they – we – will be presented to God as blameless (pure) and above reproach (without criticism). This does not mean believers never sin, but that their sins are forgiven and not counted against them. In this we can have great hope!

1. Is there anyone you pray for regularly, as Paul prayed, to grow in wisdom, spiritual understanding, and increasing knowledge of God? Does anyone pray these blessings for you? Is there someone or a small group of people you could enter into Christian fellowship with for the purpose of praying for each other?

2. Why is Christ the hope of glory in the life of a believer? Are there any unbelievers with whom God is calling you to share the mystery of this hope of glory?

COLOSSIANS, CHAPTER 2

BACKGROUND

Laodicea was founded in the third century B.C. by Antiochus II Theos, king of Syria and named in honor of his wife Laodice. Its location on the crossroads of north-south traffic (between Sardis and Perga) and east-west traffic (between Euphrates and Ephesus) allowed it to become one of the wealthiest cities of its time. Laodicea was located eleven miles north west of Colossae. It is the seventh of the seven churches mentioned in the book of Revelation (3.14-21). Hierapolis (4.13) was located in the same vicinity.

OVERVIEW

As the fruits of Paul's ministry continued to spread, he felt burdened for believers he had never met. Paul wanted these believers who had never seen him to be encouraged, united in love, and full of wisdom and knowledge. Though Paul was with them in spirit even as he was absent in the flesh, he wanted to ensure these new believers were not deceived by false teachings.

Paul used four words to describe how the Colossians should walk with Christ. The first, *rooted,* is in the past tense meaning it has already taken place. The other three, *built up, established,* and *abounding,* though not so obvious in English, are in the present tense in Greek, indicating that continual growth is a part of the Christian life.

Philosophy was prominent in the ancient world, and there were some who were mixing philosophy with the Christian faith to produce a belief system that required more than Christ's death and resurrection for salvation. Paul warned against believing in such teachings and thereby being cheated out of what had already been gained and was sufficient.

The use of the phrase *Godhead bodily*, affirms Christ's incarnation.

Spiritual circumcision, in which sin was removed from the heart, replaced circumcision of the flesh.

Baptism quickly became symbolic of Christ's death on the cross. Immersion in water symbolized *dying* with Christ while coming out of the water symbolized the believer's *resurrection* in Christ. Baptism on its own had no ability to bring salvation.

Written code or *handwriting of requirements* is a business term that referred to a debt or IOU. Paul used the term to refer to the debt all people owe God as a result of their sin. Not only were believers' sins forgiven but the rules that were established to condemn them were also rendered worthless by Christ's death.

Principalities and powers refer to Satan and his demons.

Reward referred to God's blessings. Adherence to false teachings would prevent one from receiving (*cheat them out of)* the blessing and even eternal life that results from faith in Christ.

The head was thought to be the source of life for the rest of the body. Paul used this as a metaphor for Christ, who, as the head, provides life for all believers.

Paul warned that becoming bound to rituals and laws might give the appearance of being wise, but ultimately such practices would not remove the indulgences (sins or desires) of the flesh.

INSIGHTS

Through the centuries, many people have taught falsely that more than belief in Christ's death and resurrection is required to receive salvation. Judaizers thought circumcision, the Jewish dietary laws and festivals were required, while Gnostics thought salvation came through acquiring knowledge concerning the mysteries of the universe. Paul's warning not to be bound by what Christ has already freed believers from is equally applicable today. Careful discernment will help believers see through false teachings and continue to rest in the powerful, freeing and true salvation of Jesus Christ.

1. How does Christ, who controls all rule and power, make you complete? Why are there some people who, as Paul states, adhere to the principles of the world and want to cheat believers out of the completeness found in Christ?

2. What things around you have the paragraph appearance of wisdom but really have no value in Christ? Are you allowing the world to impose requirement on you from which you have already been freed in Christ? How is Christ calling you to live in His power and provision?

Colossians, Chapter 3

BACKGROUND

To the woman he said, '... Your desire will be for your husband, and he will rule over you.' (Gen. 3.16) The man's command to rule over the wife as part of his punishment for sinning is often overlooked. Man was not created originally to rule over woman. They were stewards of the earth, together empowered to subdue chaos. Paul put the husband-wife relationship back in the proper perspective of loving stewards, not ruler and ruled.

OVERVIEW

Paul followed up the doctrinal issues he addressed in chapter 2 with practical applications in this chapter.

Instead of focusing on the temporal realm of false teachings, Paul instructed his readers to focus on the things of Christ.

The Greek word translated *hidden* denotes something that was achieved in the past and, therefore, is a present reality.

A common belief in Paul's time was that the soul was heavenly and eternal while the body was earthly, perishable and unimportant. This led to the false notion that what one did with one's body was unimportant. Paul countered this notion by listing various practices (vs. 5, 8, 9) that should not be engaged in by Christ's followers. He referred to sinful passions as members of the body that needed to be put to death.

The *old man* refers to the unredeemed life prior to placing one's faith in Christ while the *new man* refers to the new life one finds in

God through Christ. All people, regardless of their background, ethnic heritage, or cultural tradition are equal in Christ.

Paul countered the vices he listed earlier with a list of virtues that were to be a part of every believer's life. Chief among those virtues was forgiveness. It was only through the forgiveness of one's sins that salvation had been possible, therefore, extending forgiveness to others was a given.

All things should be motivated by love, which ties everything together.

If the peace of God ruled in one's heart, there would be a greater chance of unity pervading the body of believers.

Christ's word is full of wisdom and provides the basis for encouraging others in their new life in Christ.

As a summary, Paul stated that all things, whether said or done, should be done in ways befitting Christ.

Life in Christ was not just about what believers said or did but how they related to those around them, particularly in family and work relationships.

A wife's submission to her husband was not to be blind obedience but a voluntary surrender that allowed the two to work in partnership. A husband's love for his wife should lead him to seek what is best for her, not to satisfy his own welfare. A child's obedience to his/her parents in *all things* does not extend to sinful and immoral acts. A father's (parent's) discipline should be done in the spirit God uses when disciplining and teaching His children (believers).

Paul stated that eternal rewards were not just for spiritual practices but for all work that honors Christ.

The chapter break between 3 and 4 occurs at an unfortunate spot. The first verse of chapter 4 belongs with verses 22-25 of chapter 3 and finishes the relational admonitions Paul was writing to the believers in Colossae.

INSIGHTS

Though slaves and bondservants are no longer condoned today, the principles still apply. Workers are to work well for their employers as if they were working for God, not just when the boss is watching, Employers are to treat their workers fairly and without taking advantage of them. For both parties it can be easy to rationalize behavior that is not ethical, fair or just. Yet God calls both sides to refrain from excuses and to engage in their dealings with the other as if God were physically present. For all of us, this can be challenging, but we can find hope in knowing God never calls us to something we cannot accomplish.

1. What does it mean to set your mind on things above? How is your life hidden with Christ in God?

2. Paul reminded his readers that there are no divisions of any kind within the body of Christ. How do we tend to segregate ourselves into *us* and *them* today? What divisions do you see around you: rich vs. poor, educated vs. uneducated, employed vs. unemployed, this side of town vs. that side of town, and others? How can you strive to fully embrace all believers as brothers and sisters in Christ and unbelievers as potential brothers and sisters?

Colossians, Chapter 4

BACKGROUND

Distrust, suspicion and contempt of the Christian community were widespread in ancient times. Christians were considered atheists because they didn't worship the Roman gods, unpatriotic because they wouldn't burn incense to the emperor, and potentially cannibals because they ate and drank the body and blood of Jesus.

OVERVIEW

Paul encouraged the Colossians to diligently continue being thankful and praying. His request for their prayers was not that he would be freed from the difficulty he faced (prison), but that he would have more opportunities to share the good news of Christ.

Paul encouraged the believers at Colossae to counter the common misgivings felt toward them by using wisdom to make the most of the opportunities they had with unbelievers (outsiders).

Seasoned with salt meant the believers were to be interesting, engaging, and tasteful. The believers were to speak with grace and in a manner appropriate to their audience.

Tychicus was a fellow minister who accompanied Paul on part of his third missionary journey. He was sent, along with Onesimus, to deliver Paul's letter to the Colossians and answer their questions about him. Onesimus was a runaway slave Paul converted and encouraged to return to his master (see Philemon).

Paul sent greetings from both Gentile and Jewish co-workers. This would have been much more significant for the first readers of Paul's letter than for modern day readers. Aristarchus was from Thessalonica and began accompanying Paul during his third missionary journey. Mark is the gospel writer who Paul refused to take on his second missionary journey. At some point the two reconciled their differences since Paul commends him. Epaphras was from Colossae and maintained his desire to see his fellow believers grow in the Lord. Luke is the writer of both Acts and the gospel named for him. He traveled with Paul during several of his missionary journeys. Demas would later forsake Paul (2 Tim. 4.10).

Because letter delivery was more difficult in ancient times, letters were often written to be read by multiple groups of people. In this case, Paul intended his letter to the Colossians to be read by the believers in Laodicea as well. Many have speculated as to the identity of the letter to the Laodiceans, suggesting it may be one of Paul's other epistles in the New Testament. It is quite possible the letter was lost.

Archippus was a believer who likely ministered in Colossae. Paul encouraged him to continue the ministry to which God had called him.

Paul used a secretary or scribe to write his letters but was in the habit of including a portion he wrote himself as a means of personalizing and authenticating his letters (1 Cor. 16.21; Gal. 6.11; 2 Thess. 3.17; Philem. 19).

INSIGHTS

Paul's advice to be *seasoned with salt* is worth heeding today. Witnessing to non-believers by "hitting them over the head" with the gospel seldom causes them to come to faith. Far more effective is a witness that is tender, filled with grace, engaging, and spoken in a manner relevant to life's circumstances. God always wants us to speak the truth, but He also calls us to speak it with love. It can be worth recalling our own conversion experience and considering what was effective and ineffective in causing us to hear the words of hope contained in the gospel message. We can then do likewise for the unbelievers we know.

1. Paul counseled the Colossians to speak with grace in interesting, engaging and tasteful ways. How do your words come across to other people? Do you extend grace during misunderstandings or difficult situations? Is there a need to temper your words to be more Christ-like as you interact with others?

2. Paul was able to count on a few fellow believers to provide comfort during his imprisonment. Is there anyone who can count on your support regardless of the trials they face? Are you willing to walk with others as they experience hardship and suffering in their own life?

PASTORAL EPISTLES

The Pastoral Epistles, 1 and 2 Timothy and Titus, designate three of the four letters Paul wrote to individuals (Philemon is the fourth). They are called Pastoral Epistles because they were written to *pastors* or leaders of church bodies.

The word *pastor* originally referred to someone who "pastured" or shepherded a flock of sheep or other grazing animals. Guiding, protecting, feeding and caring for animals became a metaphor for the responsibilities of a leader of God's people. God Himself is referred to as the Shepherd of His people (Gen. 48:15; Ps 23:1) as were some of Israel's kings and other leaders (Jer. 23:1-4; Ezek. 34:1-31). Jesus spoke of Himself as the Good Shepherd (John 10:1-18), and several of His parables were about shepherds and sheep (Matt 18:12-14; 25:31-33). Thus, as pastoral epistles, these letters give instruction concerning the qualifications and responsibilities of people leading and caring for congregations. In addition, they include doctrinal, organizational and personal direction.

FIRST TIMOTHY

The relationship between Paul and Timothy began as early as Paul's first missionary trip when he visited Lystra, the city in which Timothy lived. As Paul preached the gospel, Timothy may have heard the message and become a believer. Though this cannot be known with certainty, we do know that Timothy accompanied Paul on his second missionary journey (Acts 16.1-3). The relationship between the two men continued to grow and Timothy became one of Paul's most trusted co-laborers in the gospel. Timothy served as Paul's representative when he could not be present and eventually was left in charge of the church in Ephesus. First Timothy was Paul's letter of encouragement to his trusted *spiritual* son.

Because Timothy was a mature believer leading a church in Ephesus, the letter does not develop doctrine as much as it reminds its reader of the importance of adhering to the doctrines that had earlier been taught. Paul included instruction on recognizing and developing Godly leadership within the church as well as recognizing and combating false doctrines that were permeating the area at the time.

First Timothy can be divided into three parts. The first, chapter 1, focuses on personal encouragement. The second part, chapters 2-3, highlights the work of ministry while the remaining chapters, 4-6, stress the duties of ministers.

1 Timothy, Chapter 1

BACKGROUND

In ancient times, personal letters were often written not only for the addressee but also with the intent of being published or read to others. As a result, such letters might include information the recipient knew because it was intended to serve as a confirmation to those who would hear the contents at a later date.

OVERVIEW

True son referred to a child who was fully a part of a family unit, including all rights and privileges. Paul used the term to indicate his confidence in Timothy as a believer.

One of the reasons Paul left Timothy in Ephesus was to correct false doctrine.

Fables/myths may have referred to Jewish fables (Tit. 1.14) while genealogies may have been used in the context of the Law (Tit. 3.9). This has led some to speculate that the false doctrines Timothy was combating were Jewish in nature.

Idle or *meaningless* talk referred to gossip, speculation and criticism, which have no place in the life of the believer.

The *teachers of the law* were those who were promoting false doctrines. Paul accused them of not fully understanding what they were teaching.

The purpose of the law was to make people aware of their sinfulness.

Those who had been made righteous through Christ were not to come under the bondage of the law.

The violations listed appear to parallel the Ten Commandments. The first four pairs recall the first five commandments. The remaining seven items parallel commandments six through nine. The last commandment (covetousness) is not mentioned.

Paul referred to the *glorious* gospel because of its message that, unlike the law, salvation is available through belief in Jesus Christ.

Paul recognized that he had once been one of the blasphemers or false teachers whom he now condemned. He felt sincere gratitude to God because it was His grace and mercy that enabled (strengthened) Paul to understand and believe in the true faith.

Paul used three words to describe what kind of sinner he had been. As a blasphemer he spoke against God. As persecutor, he pursued Christians to kill them, and as an insolent man Paul acted out of arrogance and personal pride. For these transgressions Paul counted himself as the chief sinner, yet because Christ came to save sinners, grace and mercy had been extended even to him.

Timothy apparently received some prophecies about his ministry early, which, though known to at least Timothy and Paul, are not recorded. Paul encouraged Timothy to stay true to those prophecies.

Paul used the visual image of a shipwreck to describe the destruction that occurs in the life of those who reject the faith.

Paul's delivery of Hymenaeus and Alexander to Satan was a means of acknowledging the path they had already chosen to take, rather than a pronouncement of judgment. Paul hoped the men would learn not to speak against God and thereby be restored to the faith.

INSIGHTS

The *exceedingly abundant* grace Paul recognized God had given him was not reserved for Paul alone. Grace is the daily, undeserved favor of God given to those who rightfully deserve judgment. God warned that the penalty of sin would be death. He could have stopped there, allowing all who sinned to experience the just penalty. In His mercy, however, He permitted sinners an opportunity to experience redemption instead of judgment. Eternal life and eternal death are at opposite ends of a spectrum and by permitting believers to move from one end to the other, God extended exceedingly abundant grace.

1. Paul wrote this letter to Timothy in order to instruct and encourage him. Who is God calling you to invest time in, to instruct and encourage as they minister to others?

2. When Paul persecuted early believers, He stood against everything Christ stood for. That did not prevent Jesus from forgiving Paul, calling Paul, and using Paul for His purposes. Are you allowing anything to stand in the way of perceiving God's forgiveness? Have you judged your past is beyond God's redemption when God has already forgiven you and is waiting to use you for His purposes?

BACKGROUND

Rome allowed its subject people to continue in their native worship practices providing they showed their loyalty to Rome. Worshipping the goddess Roma and making sacrifices to the spirit of the emperor accomplished this. The Jews were able to gain Roman approval to make sacrifices *for* the emperor's health rather than *to* him because of their exclusive worship of one God. Regular prayers in the synagogues also served to confirm Jewish loyalty to Roman rule.

OVERVIEW

Paul's exhortation to pray includes four types of prayers. *Supplication* or *requests* includes the idea of petitioning for personal needs. *Prayers* as used in the scriptures is the general term for prayer and is always directed to God. *Intercession* suggests praying on behalf of another and is the opposite of supplication. *Giving thanks* or *thanksgiving* includes an attitude of praising God for what He has done.

Praying for kings and others in authority was motivated by two ideas. First, the leadership of the nation had an impact on society as a whole. Thus praying for the leaders by extension meant praying for all people. Second, it serves as a reminder that God is in control and can affect people and events at the highest level.

Mediator comes from the Old Testament concept of the priests serving as mediators between God and the people through the sacrifices they offered to atone for sin.

Paul was well aware of his calling to preach the truth to the Gentiles and it was no doubt this that motivated him to leave Timothy in Ephesus to combat the false teachings that were circulating at the time.

Just as men were to be sincere and authentic when they prayed, women were to be modestly dressed. The emphasis was to be on prayer, not on attracting or distracting others through one's apparel and hair decorations (which could be very elaborate in ancient times).

Paul's restrictions on women in the church were not likely based on their gender; he did not restrict women praying or prophesying as long as they were dressed appropriately (1 Cor. 11.4-5), and he recognized a number of women who had been invaluable to the growth of the church (Rom. 16.1-5).

Given that most women in ancient Jewish and Roman culture were not encouraged to and had little to no opportunity to learn, Paul's words should not be taken as restricting women from learning. Rather, he was setting parameters for and encouraging the education of women in a culture that was unaccustomed to doing so. Silence and submission were designed to keep the assemblies focused and from becoming unruly.

Paul's admonition that women not teach men or have authority over them seems harsh by today's standards. This section of scripture has caused much debate and controversy over the centuries. Some believe the restriction is absolute and clear in meaning. Others believe the admonition must be taken in the cultural context in which it was written. Women were not educated. Many had come from pagan backgrounds and had not yet learned the doctrines of their new faith. As a result, they would have been susceptible to believing many of the false teachings that were circulating. Paul encouraged them to learn but not to teach to prevent the further spread of those teachings that were contrary to the good news of the gospel.

INSIGHTS

Many of Paul's admonitions concerning women were written with a focus on motive. What was a woman's motive for how she dressed or what she did? The question applies equally to men. God is much more concerned with our inside appearance than our outward appearance. Much of our inside appearance is determined by our motives. Is our motive to receive accolades from people or commendation from God? God has defined what is necessary to receive His blessings and what happens when we seek the praises of people. It is up to us to choose between the two and enjoy or suffer the consequences that result.

1. Are the four prayers Paul mentioned a regular part of your prayer life? Do you pray with confidence in the power and authority given to you by Jesus?

2. Do you pray for the wisdom and good leadership of those in authority over you, whether you agree with their politics or not?

1 TIMOTHY, CHAPTER 3

BACKGROUND

The two offices of the early church, bishop (overseer) and deacon, were designed to care for all the needs of the Christian community while not burdening one office with more than could be accommodated. The bishop was charged with preaching the gospel and leading and caring for the people. The Greek word for deacon means *servant* and likely referred to a calling that was more administrative in nature.

OVERVIEW

Paul's instructions next turned to those who led the Ephesian church. Bishops were akin to pastors today. They were charged with leading and caring for the local body of Christ.

Paul listed sixteen qualifications a man must meet in order to serve in the position of bishop. The list was not intended to be exhaustive, though gave a well-rounded list of the requirements.

The general consensus on *husband of one wife* (also applicable to deacons) is that a man can be legitimately divorced and remarried and adhere to the requirement. Some believe the requirement disqualifies anyone who has divorced and remarried. The requirement disqualifies those who are sexually immoral or polygamists.

Most of the requirements refer to a person's character, having self-control, integrity, and proper priorities. The second to last requirement ensured the person had reached a level of maturity in his faith before being placed in a position in which he was responsible for training and growing others.

A bishop's good reputation in the secular community ensured a good testimony to nonbelievers and helped to avoid the work of Satan having any effect.

The requirements for deacons were similar to those of bishops. Deacons who served well were encouraged on two fronts. First, they would enjoy good standing (respect, reward) both among their fellow believers and at the judgment seat of Christ. Second, they would gain confidence and assurance as they continued their walk with Christ.

There are two general interpretations of *likewise, their wives* . . . Some believe Paul was referring to the wives of male deacons, while others contend the *likewise* used to introduce deacons is used a second time to introduce a third church office of deaconess. Documents from ancient Rome attest to the role of deaconesses in the church as early as 112 A.D.

The early church met in local houses (thus, house of God), which made up the universal and collective church (church of the living God).

The final verse of this chapter is thought to include an early church hymn.

INSIGHTS

Of all the qualifications Paul listed for bishops, deacons and deaconesses (or deacon's wives), only two do not necessarily apply to all believers. Bishops needed the ability to teach, which may or may not be a spiritual gift of individual believers. Neither were they to be novices when assigned to their position, though they and all believers start as novices and grow in maturity. All believers, however, can and should strive to live in a manner that would qualify them for leadership in the church. This does not mean all believers are called or should strive to be leaders in the church but that they live such impeccable lives they could be leaders.

1. Are you living your life in such a way that if your body of believers called upon you to serve, you would meet the spiritual qualifications outlined by Paul?

2. What things are you doing to ensure that you grow in spiritual maturity?

1 TIMOTHY, CHAPTER 4

BACKGROUND

Timothy was not the only person in scripture encouraged to do as God called him to do despite objections about his young age. God called Jeremiah at an early age. When Jeremiah protested that he was too young to do as God commanded, God promised He would be with Jeremiah in all he did and deliver him from the trials he would face (Jer. 1).

OVERVIEW

Having completed his instructions for the church leadership, Paul turned to instructions specifically for Timothy.

The prophecy to which Paul refers is uncertain. He may mean a particular revelation he received for Timothy or he may be referring to general prophecies directed at those who abandon God's truth (Matt. 24.4-12).

Continually choosing to sin will eventually result in a conscience that no longer warns against wrongdoing. Paul suggests that a hot iron has numbed such consciences.

All of God's creation is declared to be *very good* (Gen. 1.31). Believers are to enjoy and be thankful for the things God created because they are good, not abstain because a false teacher declared them to be other than good.

Paul encouraged Timothy to teach the doctrine he himself had learned. Doing so would edify those he taught and provide continued nourishment and reinforcement for himself.

Just as an athlete engages in physical exercise, so a believer should engage in spiritual exercise. Such exercise will lead to living a godly life. Physical exercise is beneficial only for a short time, but spiritual exercise benefits believers for their entire earthly lives as well as their eternal lives.

All people experience God's common grace while only those who believe in His Son experience His saving grace.

Youth could be applied to anyone up to forty years old, though more frequently was applied to those under twenty-nine. Timothy's age at the time Paul wrote this letter is unknown. He could have been as young as his mid-twenties or as old as his mid-thirties.

It is likely Timothy was younger than at least some of the people to whom he was ministering. Paul was confident in Timothy's ability and encouraged him not to be intimidated because of his age. Paul listed six areas in which he was to set an example: word (dialogue), conduct, love (reflecting God's love), spirit (empowerment by the Holy Spirit), faith, and purity (in how he lived and what he thought).

Timothy was to pay special attention to three areas as he ministered in the Ephesian church: reading the scriptures in public, preaching (exhortation), and teaching (doctrine). These three would encourage and mature the believers in the body as well as correct any false teachings that were circulating.

Laying on of hands was used to commission believers for service in church offices as well as recognize God's work and calling in their lives.

Save was not a suggestion that Timothy could achieve salvation by what he did. Rather, it was more along the lines of encouraging believers in their daily walk with Christ.

INSIGHTS

Without a doubt, believers are to enjoy what God has created. It should be noted, however, that such enjoyment should not be motivated by a desire for self-indulgent pleasure. All of creation has a spiritual side. God designed marriage to reflect the fellowship and intimacy of the Godhead. Possessions are given to believers to steward on God's behalf and use to fulfill His purposes. Food is to be enjoyed, yet provides nourishment and health to the body thereby enabling the believer to carry out God's will. Whether we experience abundance or lack of these things, God desires us to be content and walk in deep intimacy with Him.

1. How can you guard against abandoning your faith in Christ due to deceiving spirits and teachings of hypocritical liars whom the Holy Spirit through Paul warned about? What role does relationship with other believers play in being alert to such deception?

2. Paul encouraged Timothy to train himself to be godly. Today, what would such training look like? What training can you put in place to ensure you are godly?

1 Timothy, Chapter 5

BACKGROUND

In the first century, wine was made by allowing grapes to ferment; a process that began almost immediately after they were picked because no type of refrigeration was available. The resulting liquid was mixed with one or two parts of water. Wine accompanied meals, and was often taken for medicinal purposes. It was particularly helpful in settling stomach issues and helped prevent dysentery by killing germs in water.

OVERVIEW

In this chapter, Paul gave Timothy instructions on various relationships, including old and young men, old and young women, widows and elders.

Rebuke means to speak to someone harshly. Those who were older than Timothy were to be treated with respect just as he would treat his parents. Those younger were to be treated as siblings.

Honor was shown both through one's treatment of another and the financial support one offered.

Paul's reference to those who were *really widows* or *widows really in need* meant those women who had no other family to support them.

Paul instructed families to care for members in need. Doing so would *repay* the time and energy parents invested in raising their children. Widows who chose to *live in pleasure* focused on their own needs. They were dead because they were separated from fellowship with God and other believers.

Family members who refused to help their own (near family) or their household (immediate family) were doing the equivalent of rejecting their faith.

Put on the list or *taken into the number* referred to the list of widows the church supported. The list may have been an order of widows who engaged in charity and prayer.

Sixty years may be the actual age or mean when old age begins.

Some have suggested that being the *wife of one husband* meant being faithful to one's husband and could include being married more than once.

Paul's concern for younger widows was that they have enough to do. Remarrying and bearing children would save them from the temptation to do things they should not. It would also reinforce their own faith as well as allow them to continue providing a good testimony to their faith.

Elders who preached and taught the scriptures well (labored in word and doctrine) were worthy of double honor, meaning they should be treated with respect and paid adequately for their efforts to care for the church. To back up his claim, Paul quoted two verses, Deut. 25.4 and Luke 10.7.

Old Testament law required the word of two or three witnesses in order for a testimony to be valid (Deut. 19.15). Paul applied the same mandate to accusations brought against elders. Rumors or the opinion of one person were not adequate to bring a charge of wrongdoing.

A public rebuke was not only intended to cause repentance in the elder sinning but to dissuade other elders from sinning.

Church discipline was important and had to be administered without personal bias or discriminatory treatment.

Timothy was to avoid becoming impure himself by not restoring a fallen leader too quickly to leadership.

Both sins and good deeds that were not evident at the time they were done would be revealed at the final judgment.

INSIGHTS

Paul's advice that Timothy approach all things without prejudice and partiality is worth adhering to today. It can be very easy to get caught up in personal preferences, returning favors and unwarranted judgments that cloud how we think and act toward others. God's desire is that we set aside our own biases, the gain we might realize, or the undeserved judgments we make and treat each person fairly and equally. We can be especially motivated to do this when we realize that God has promised to judge us in the same way we have judged others (Matt. 7.2).

1. How might the world change if all people treated those older then themselves as parents and those younger as siblings and particularly younger women with purity? Is there anything in your behavior toward others that needs to change in order to take Paul's appeal to heart?

2. Paul encouraged Timothy to let his good deeds speak for themselves, trusting that those not easily seen would not forever remain hidden. When do you seek personal accolades for the good deeds you do? Can you be content to let such deeds speak for themselves whenever it is they might become known?

1 Timothy, Chapter 6

BACKGROUND

Jesus gave twice as many references to money (including talents, riches and treasure) than to whom and how to love. Money in and of itself is not evil. Rather it is the love of money and the pursuit of it to the exclusion of higher priorities that both Jesus and Paul warned against. Money is a tool that, like many other tools, should be seen for what it is and used wisely.

OVERVIEW

Believing slaves were to treat their unbelieving masters with respect. Their attitude and actions toward their masters were to serve as a witness to the presence and power of Christ in their lives with the hope that the master would be drawn into the same faith. Believing slaves of believing masters were not to despise their masters but to serve them well; confident that the whole body of Christ would benefit.

False teachers were those who taught other than the truth of the gospel message of Christ. Such teachers were often more interested in debating word meanings and how they might personally gain than they were in the truth.

Contentment is feeling satisfied with what one has rather than continually striving for more. Godliness encompasses more than being devout or religious. It is realized as one enters into communion with God Himself (John 17:3). Paul offered one reason for being content and that is that everyone eventually dies. All s/he accumulates during a lifetime is left behind and of no value in the judgment, and life to come.

Food and clothing represent the most basic of needs and it is with these that believers are to find contentment.

Paul warned against desiring to be rich. There is nothing wrong with money, but the love and pursuit of money leads to temptations one would not experience otherwise. These powerful temptations can ultimately drown (literally drag down) and destroy a person.

Timothy was to run away from those temptations that could destroy him and seek instead those things that were beneficial to him. Of the items Paul listed, three are character qualities (righteousness, godliness, and faith) while three are part of the fruit of the Spirit (love, patience, and gentleness; Gal. 5.22).

Pontius Pilate said of Jesus, *I find no fault in this Man* (Luke 23.4). Paul urged Timothy to live in such a way that he would have a similar pronouncement.

Timothy was to be motivated by the return of Christ, not by greed and what he could accumulate during his lifetime.

Paul interrupted his exhortations with a doxology to Christ.

Paul wanted those who were wealthy to be rich spiritually as well. Spiritual wealth comes from using what God has given to help those who are in need.

Timothy had been entrusted with the truth of the gospel, which he was to guard with all diligence. Failure to do so would lead to practices that had caused others to abandon the faith.

Paul ended his letter as he began by praying for God's grace upon Timothy and those who read the letter (the you in Greek is plural).

INSIGHTS

Living a godly, contented life can provide as much gain for us today as it did for Timothy. The world bombards us with messages that more is better, enough is never enough, and winning comes from getting. Yet what the world doesn't tell us is that all the *things* that are supposed to bring us satisfaction never do. There is a place where enough *is* enough and generally it is long before the world believes it is true. Anyone who is unconvinced need only look at the lives of some movie stars. Many are filled with pain, brokenness, disappointment and divorce as they strive after a sense of fulfillment that comes only through godly contentment.

1. Godliness with contentment is great gain is a verse that is often quoted. What does it mean? How can you learn to be content? Why does Paul warn so strongly against wanting to be rich?

2. We, like Timothy, are called by God to guard what has been entrusted to our care. Who (children, spouse, students, subordinates, neighbors, parents) or what (time, talents, abilities, possessions, money) have been entrusted into your care? How do you guard them well? Is there anyone or anything you need to release to God and take on the role of steward rather than owner?

SECOND TIMOTHY

Paul was eventually released from the house arrest under which he was held when he wrote 1 Timothy (and Titus). When the great fire in Rome broke out, completely destroying four of fourteen districts and severely damaging seven more, rumors began to spread that the emperor, Nero, had deliberately set the fire to make way for the series of palaces he planned to build. Though it seems unlikely that Nero set the fire, he attempted to improve public opinion of himself by spreading his own rumors that the Christians had started it. The plan worked and Nero began a period of intense persecution aimed at Christians.

It was in this environment that Paul again found himself in prison. The second time he was in a cold, dark prison cell, wanting a cloak to keep warm and waiting for his pending execution, not under house arrest with the freedom to receive guests. (Peter was also in Rome during this period and according to tradition was eventually crucified upside down at his own request.)

Knowing that his life would soon end, Paul wrote his final letter, this one to his beloved *son,* Timothy. This letter was written approximately four years after the first and in many ways serves as Paul's final will and testament. Paul had been abandoned by many of his friends, some of whom had left the faith entirely. Though Luke remained with Paul, Paul longed to see his *spiritual son* one last time. Sensing that Timothy might not be able to make the journey in time, Paul included instructions and encouragement for Timothy, who was himself experiencing persecution as he continued to lead the church in Ephesus.

Second Timothy can be divided into four parts along chapter lines. In the first chapter, Paul encouraged Timothy to persevere in the faith. In the second, Paul used three examples to illustrate the hardships faced and persistence needed to live the gospel. Chapter three dealt with facing apostasy and persecution while the last chapter again encouraged Timothy to preach the faith he knew to be true.

2 Timothy, Chapter 1

BACKGROUND

In the first century a day was measured from sundown to sundown. Thus *night and day* placed the periods in their natural order.

The *forefathers* would have been a reference to Abraham, Isaac and Jacob. They are the patriarchs of the Jewish faith. Since Christianity is rooted in the promises made to the Jewish people, Abraham, Isaac and Jacob are viewed as patriarchs to the Christian faith as well.

OVERVIEW

Paul stated he was *an apostle . . . according to the promise of life.* He wrote those words as he sat in prison awaiting his own execution.

Timothy's mother was a Jewish believer by the time Paul met her (Acts 16.1). It would appear that his grandmother was also.

God, through the workings of the Holy Spirit, empowers believers to do His will. Because of this, believers can have confidence in Him and replace their fear with power, love and self-discipline (self-control or sound mind).

Paul wanted Timothy to have confidence in the gospel despite the persecution that pervaded the empire. Paul's imprisonment was just one example of the suffering that was a part of believing in Christ and sharing the gospel message.

God's call on believers' lives was neither haphazard nor impulsive but was planned before the beginning of creation.

By destroying death and bringing immortality, Jesus removed any reason to fear death that believers might experience when they proclaim the truth of the gospel.

Paul himself modeled the confidence he wanted Timothy to have in the gospel. Even though Paul was in prison and had suffered repeatedly for the sake of the gospel, he was completely confident in God and His promises.

Sound words referred to the gospel truth Timothy had been taught. Paul commanded him to hold onto or keep these truths by living them. The truths did not originate with Paul but came through the Holy Spirit who lives in all believers.

As Paul lamented those who had abandoned him, he pointed to one who had not been ashamed and continued to minister to Paul, even as he suffered in prison.

Onesiphorus means *help bringer.*

INSIGHTS

In the Christian faith, life is more than our physical lives, which are temporary. It is also eternal life, which is never ending. Though we can only begin to imagine what eternal life will look like, there are enough references in the Bible to indicate that it will be beyond our imagination. God has great plans for those who believe in Him and the saving grace of His Son. Suffering in this life is a part of the gospel and should be expected by every believer, but suffering will not be a part of our eternal lives (Rev. 21:4). In this we can place great hope, even as our current experiences might leave us feeling there is no hope.

1. With so much of the world opposed to the Christian faith, we can find ourselves ashamed to testify to the truth of Christ. How do we join in the suffering of the gospel by the power of God? (1.8) Even in the midst of hostility, how can we reflect the grace of Christ back to the world?

2. Is there anyone you can count on, as Paul was able to count on Onesiphorus? Is there anyone who can count on you in the same manner? If not, what can you do to foster such a relationship with one or two other believers?

2 Timothy, Chapter 2

BACKGROUND

Gnosticism refers to a wide variety of beliefs that were prevalent in the second century A.D., though some roots can be found in the first century B.C. The principle belief centered on special knowledge that was required to achieve salvation. In addition, some Gnostics believed that what was done with the body had no effect on the soul (often leading to a licentious lifestyle) or that the body was evil and needed discipline. Evidence of combating gnostic thought can be found in some of Paul's writings.

OVERVIEW

Paul had seen many he thought faithful turn away from him and the faith he taught. He exhorted Timothy to remain strong in Christ. The emphasis is on Christ, who provides the strength to do what humans cannot do on their own.

Paul encouraged Timothy to pass the gospel message on to faithful believers who would, in turn, pass it on to other faithful believers.

Paul used three illustrations to show some of the qualities Timothy should pursue as a faithful believer.

- Soldiers were devoted to their service with such single-mindedness that they did not engage in many day-to-day activities.

- Athletes trained and competed in order to wear the victor's crown but did so only by being faithful to the rules of the competition.

- Farmers were able to harvest a crop only after much hard work.

Jesus the *seed of David* emphasizes Jesus' humanity while His resurrection emphasizes the fulfillment of God's plan for salvation.

Paul found his hope, his ability to endure his circumstances, from his confidence in God's Word and promises.

Verses 11-13 may be a quote from an early hymn or statement of faith. The last part of the statement is worth noting. God's covenant is not dependent upon the faithfulness of human beings. In the midst of human unfaithfulness, God remains faithful.

Paul encouraged Timothy not to get into petty debates over insignificant words. Side issues can never be as important as God's truths.

Paul twice warned Timothy to beware of Hymenaeus. The first time in conjunction with Alexander (1 Tim. 1.20) and in this letter with Philetus. These men were teaching that the resurrection was spiritual in nature and had already occurred. Their false teaching was having a detrimental effect on some believers.

Paul figuratively referred to human beings as vessels. Some believers, spoken of as gold and silver vessels, are useful to God while others, described as wood and clay, were not so useful. Whether Paul was comparing the righteous to the wicked or believers who have purified themselves through repentance to those who have not purified themselves is unclear. Whichever interpretation was intended, Paul was warning Timothy to pursue those things that would make him useful to God.

One aim of those who serve God is to correct the false thinking of those who oppose the gospel. Such correction must be done with humility and without quarreling. The aim is to bring such people to repentance, that they may know God's truth and be saved from the workings and purposes of Satan.

INSIGHTS

Paul's illustrations for character qualities of believers still apply today. God desires believers to single-mindedly pursue His truths (Matt. 6.33); to strive for the crown of life by being faithful to God's truth (Jam. 1.12), and participate in the harvest of believers through work that often is hard (Matt. 9.37). Just as with any character quality, these can be developed through reading and studying God's Word, spiritual disciplines (prayer, fasting, silence, solitude, etc.) and using one's spiritual gifts to serve others.

1. Paul stated that even though he was chained in prison, God's word was not. What circumstances, even those that are unpleasant, can you use to testify to the love, truth and grace of Jesus Christ?

2. Paul encouraged Timothy to clean house; to rid himself of anything, regardless of value, that served a less than godly purpose. Is there anything in your possession that served or serves an ungodly purpose? Would you get rid of it in order to be noble, holy, useful, and prepared for whatever God calls you to?

2 Timothy, Chapter 3

BACKGROUND

In ancient times women were often more susceptible to false teaching because they lacked education. Married Greek women lived a partially segregated life and were rarely seen in public. As a result, false teachers had to gain access to homes in order to make contact with these women. Once there, the false teachers often obtained financial support and other assistance as well.

According to Jewish tradition and some pagan accounts, Jannes and Jambres were brothers who served as Pharaoh's magicians and opposed Moses (Ex. 7.11).

OVERVIEW

The term *last days* refers to the days before Christ's second coming. Some define this as the period immediately prior to Christ's return while others believe it encompasses all the time between when Christ first came and when He returns.

Paul listed a series of character qualities that denote those who do not follow Christ. *Having a form of godliness but denying its power* referred to those who appeared to be godly by making a show of practicing religious ritual but lack any belief in or relationship with Christ.

Though false teachers will persist for a time, God will eventually expose the error of their teaching.

Paul contrasted the qualities of those who do not follow God with qualities found in his own life as a believer and committed teacher of the gospel.

Paul virtually promises that all who fervently desire to follow Christ will suffer persecution.

Though evil and those deceived by evil would continue to grow, Paul exhorted Timothy to continue in the things he knew to be true.

All that Timothy had learned from childhood on and knew to be true came from God-inspired scripture. Paul highlighted four purposes scripture serves. The first, *doctrine* (*teaching*), is directed toward information and knowledge while the other three focus on life change. *Reproofing* (*rebuking*) and *correcting* both aim at pointing out a person's false thinking and replacing it with the truth. *Training* (*instruction*) in righteousness refers to molding one's character through proper teaching as a parent does with a child.

Through study of the scriptures, believers become capable and prepared to carry out the work God desires them to do.

INSIGHTS

Paul called the scriptures *inspired* (*God-breathed*) to show that they are the authoritative word of God. The scriptures exist not because various men chose to put thoughts on paper, but because God Himself inspired men to write His truths. In so doing, we have a record of God's interaction with His people as well as instructions and messages that are thoroughly relevant to our lives today.

1. Paul contrasted qualities found in unbelievers with those found in his life as a believer. Which qualities do you see in your own life? Are there some you would like to see as no longer part of your life? Some as more significant in your life? What might you need to seek from the Lord to make this happen?

2. Paul listed four purposes scripture serves. How do you see each of the purposes playing a role in your life? In which area do you need to allow scripture to speak a more prominent message in your life?

2 Timothy, Chapter 4

BACKGROUND

A drink offering was one of several offerings prescribed in the Old Testament. It was performed by pouring wine on the ground or altar and often accompanied a meat offering (Num. 28.14-31). It is interesting to note that Jesus is referred to as a Lamb who was slain (Rev. 5.12). Figuratively, Paul's life being poured out as a drink offering accompanied the Lamb offering made on behalf of humanity's sins.

OVERVIEW

Paul's final charge to Timothy was emphasized by calling upon God and Christ. He included a reminder that Jesus would one day return to judge all people.

Paul used *the word* almost exclusively throughout his letters to mean the truth of the gospel. Timothy's calling was to minister to and encourage both the leadership of the church at Ephesus as well as the body of believers. The basis of any ministry is the Word of God. Paul called Timothy to be ready at all times to share God's truths with those who needed to hear them and to do so with patience.

Itching ears referred to people who only wanted to hear whatever suited their present needs and wants. Paul pointed to a time when people would have no interest in the truth but would seek only that which justified their decisions and actions.

The Greek term translated as *myths (fables)* was usually used to denote false stories in a disparaging manner.

Paul used his life as an example to encourage Timothy to remain strong through to the end of his life.

Knowing his death was imminent, Paul was able to look back and see a life that had persevered in the midst of great trial and suffering in order to deliver and remain faithful to the message of Christ. He was confident that his ability to finish well would be rewarded when the Day of Judgment came.

Several references in the New Testament speak of a crown given as an eternal reward (Jam. 1.12; 1 Pet. 5.4; Rev. 2.10).

As a spiritual son, Paul had done all he could to encourage Timothy in his calling and work. Now that he was in prison, Paul desired some encouragement of his own from Timothy.

The *Mark* Paul requested Timothy to bring was most likely the Mark (sometimes referred to as John Mark) who left Paul during his first missionary journey. At the beginning of his second journey, Paul so strongly refused to travel with Mark that he and Barnabas went their separate ways (Acts 13.13; 15.36-40). This verse indicates that reconciliation between Paul and Mark had occurred.

Paul listed a number of people Timothy could look for or look out for. Some had been faithful to the gospel, while others had not.

Paul did not pray for vengeance on Alexander but that he would be judged by his deeds, just as all people will.

Though people had abandoned Paul when he stood trial, he reflected Christ by forgiving them. In spite of human failings, Paul knew he could always count on the Lord for strength.

Paul ended his letter by wishing for Timothy the gift Paul had received in greatest abundance – grace, the unmerited favor of God.

INSIGHTS

Paul's focus right up to his dying day was twofold – a yearning to see believers mature in their faith so they might ever more completely serve

Christ and a desire that those who did not know Christ would come to the saving knowledge of Him and thereby be counted as sons of God. Paul is a good model for modern day believers.

God has given all believers spiritual gifts to be used to further His purposes. There are no examples in the Bible of someone who served faithfully for a number of years and then retired from God's service. Moses, Abraham, David, Paul and many others all died striving to complete the work God had given them.

1. How can you follow Paul's prompting to Timothy to be levelheaded, willing to suffer through hardships, do the work God has called you to and fulfill your ministry to others?

2. Paul was able to look back on his life and make positive statements about the way he lived. When you approach the end of your life, what things would you hope to say about the way you lived your life? Are you on track to be able to say those things? Are there changes you need to make now in order to achieve your hopes?

TITUS

Though Titus is not mentioned in Luke's descriptions of Paul's missionary journeys found in Acts, it is evident that Titus was one of Paul's disciples. Paul mentions him thirteen times in his epistles. It is thought Titus accompanied Paul on at least a portion of his missionary journeys and was sent as Paul's representative to Corinth on as many as three occasions. Eventually, Paul left Titus at the church in Crete to bring some order and provide leadership to a church that was struggling. Just as in Ephesus, false teachers were present and attempting to take advantage of the young church by establishing false truths as doctrine.

In addition to instructions on church organization and guidelines for church leaders, Titus contains one of the most straightforward statements on God's grace found anywhere in the New Testament. The book can be divided into three parts, which parallel its three chapters. In the first chapter, Paul focused on the need for sound leadership in the Cretan church. In the second chapter, Paul gave instructions to various groups within the church. Finally, Paul emphasized the importance of good works as an outpouring of the Christian life.

Titus, Chapter 1

BACKGROUND

God cannot lie. The ninth commandment prohibits lying (bearing false witness means not telling the truth; Deut. 5.20). After the formation of the church, God's first act of discipline was against lying (Acts 5.3).

Crete is the largest of the Greek Isles and the fifth largest island in the Mediterranean. It already had a long history by the time Paul stopped there as a prisoner on his way to Rome.

OVERVIEW

The introduction Paul used here is common to his letters: he was a servant of God and an apostle of Christ.

Who cannot lie is a statement about God's character. Everything God has promised will come to pass.

Just as Paul called Timothy a true son out of great affection, so he also called Titus.

One purpose of Paul's letter was to provide Titus with instructions for finishing those things that were lacking in the church on Crete. Paul focused on three areas that needed attention: the organization of the church, the false teachers who were spreading their teaching among the believers, and the need for instruction in doctrine and application to daily life.

The words *elders* and *bishop* appear to be used interchangeably in this context.

The list of requirements for an elder or bishop defined the relationship he should have with his family (wife and children) as well as himself. Though Paul stated these as requirements for anyone who would serve in leadership within the church, they were qualities all believers should exhibit.

Paul's use of *those of the circumcision* suggests that some of the false teachers were Jews who insisted that the Jewish laws and rituals be kept in order to enjoy God's blessings.

Epimenides, a poet from approximately 600 B.C., is said to have written the words that all Cretans are liars. The extent to which this was true is unknown, though Cretans did have a reputation for being dishonest. Paul's acknowledgment that the statement was true in a letter that was likely to be read to the body of believers indicates there was at least some truth to it.

Jewish fables were likely legends about Old Testament figures that did not appear in the scriptures. From those stories, false doctrines and teachings would have been drawn and taught as truth. Those who taught or adhered to such false teachings were defiled not by what they did but by what they thought and believed.

INSIGHTS

Paul warned against those who claimed to know God but contradicted that proclamation with what they did. In modern terms, they did not walk their talk. Nothing is hidden from God. He knows all motives, actions, words and attitudes. As such, our best course of action is to be believers of integrity—to say what we do and do what we say. Not only will we avoid God's judgment, we will also give the best possible witness to non-believers.

1. What comfort does the fact that God cannot lie bring you? How can it inspire you to trust in Him more completely? What are some of the truths you can count on God to keep?

2. Paul listed essential qualities for any person considered for leadership within the church. Do you use these as a basis for selecting and/or endorsing leaders in your church today? Do you work toward these qualities being a part of your character so that if, one day, God calls you to a position of leadership, you will be ready?

BACKGROUND

God is repeatedly referred to as Savior (Is. 43.3; 45.15; Hos. 13.4; Lk. 1.47; 1 Tim. 1.1; Jude 25). As might be expected, Jesus is also referred to as Savior (Lk. 2.11; Jn. 4.42; Phil. 3.20; 2 Pt. 2.20). Paul referred to the Savior as both God and Jesus Christ (2.13), making one of the strongest statements in the New Testament concerning the deity of Christ.

OVERVIEW

The Greek word for *sound* could equally be translated *healthy*. Paul's rebuke of false teaching was followed by an exhortation on how believers should live. It is only through the right doctrine that the right way of living will be achieved.

For both men and women, *older* referred to fifty years or more. By that age (though not guaranteed) these believers should have reached a level of maturity that could serve as a model for younger, less mature believers.

Self-control (temperate) means *resisting temptation* and includes control emotionally, physically and in one's thoughts.

Blaspheme means to speak irreverently against God or sacred things. Paul warned against blaspheming against the Word of God. Since this warning follows a listing of proper ways to act, being irreverent can be demonstrated by what one does just as much as what one says.

Instructing children in the ways of God is the responsibility of every parent (Deut. 6.7; Prov. 22.6). However, such instruction does not cease when one becomes an adult. There is still more to learn, and older men and women were given the responsibility to pass on their wisdom and knowledge.

Paul reminded Titus that he must take the lead in demonstrating how one was to act. Titus' own ability to minister and teach would be compromised if he did not himself act in a manner befitting Christ.

Believing bondservants (slaves) were instructed to treat their masters well. Such behavior would serve as a good testimony for the faith to unbelieving masters.

In the last verses of this chapter (11-14), Paul made one of the most straightforward statements about God's grace found anywhere in the New Testament. In these verses Paul brings together the present, future and past. He begins by calling for godly living in the present times, then moves to the future hope believers have as a result of their faith in Christ. Finally, Paul recalls the past sacrifice made by Christ, which ultimately makes godly living in the present and hope in the future possible.

INSIGHTS

Maturity in Christ is a reflection of how well a believer is able to apply the truths of the gospel message to life. Applying such truths covers a broad range of areas such as distinguishing between right and wrong, recognizing evil, a readiness to admit wrongdoing and seek forgiveness, being quick to extend forgiveness, a willingness to speak the truth especially when it is unpopular or not well received, and a desire to seek and carry out God's will even when it includes cost or sacrifice on the part of the believer. God never promised maturing in Him would be easy, but He has promised to walk with us as we seek such maturity.

1. How can you ensure that the things you speak are of sound doctrine? What things can you do or are you doing to grow in the wisdom and knowledge of Jesus?

2. If you are a mature believer in Christ, are you seeking younger believers you can encourage and instruct? If you are a newer believer in Christ, are you seeking the wisdom and knowledge of more mature believers to help you respond appropriately to life's circumstances, events and trials?

Titus, Chapter 3

BACKGROUND

Tychicus and Apollos were co-workers of Paul's mentioned both by Luke (Acts 20.4; 18.24; 19.1) and several times by Paul in his letters (Eph. 6.21; Col. 4.7; 2 Tim 4.12; 1 Cor. 1.12; 3.4-6, 22; 4.6; 16.12). Nothing is known of the other men Paul names. Many nameless people have played a significant role in the advancement of the gospel since the time of Christ.

OVERVIEW

Paul's reminders to Titus about how the Cretans should behave was no doubt motivated by their reputation (1.12). As believers, the Cretans were called to set aside their own desires and judgments of right and wrong and be obedient to the laws and values of Jesus Christ.

God's grace had permeated the lives of the Cretans (and all believers) when they were still unbelievers. Therefore the Cretans should willingly reflect that same grace to those who had yet to know God.

Though Paul had been emphasizing the need for good works in believers' lives, he also wanted to make clear that such good works had no power to bring salvation to the unbeliever. Salvation came solely through the mercy of God when the choice to believe in His Son was made. Good works were an outpouring of that salvation as believers expressed their gratitude to God for what He had done for and in them.

Regeneration represents the rebirth Jesus spoke of (John 3.3). It is the instantaneous cleansing work of the Holy Spirit that occurs when one places his/her faith in Christ.

The Holy Spirit, given to all believers through the work of Christ, is not given sparingly or frugally but lavishly.

God's justifying work in those who believe allows them to become coheirs and rulers with Christ.

Paul reiterated the beneficial nature of good works done with the right motivation.

After stating ways in which the believing Cretans should act, Paul listed some of the practices they should avoid. Included was anything that would encourage or advance wickedness among the believers.

Those who would not admit to the need for correction after two warnings were not to be tolerated within the body of believers. Such people were steeped in rebellion toward God and unwilling to change their ways. Paul reserved the exclusion from the believing community for only the most extreme of circumstances. In many ways, the unrepentant person had already excluded him/herself from community life.

Paul ended his letter to Titus on the theme that had pervaded it: the need for good works. The display of such works by meeting the needs of others would result in being fruitful for God.

INSIGHTS

Paul's reminder that the Cretans obey the rulers and authorities set over them is worthy of noting today. Other places in scripture tell us that people are in their position of authority because God has put them there (Rom. 13.1). As long as following those in authority does not cause believers to go against one of God's commands, we are to submit to such rules and regulations. This can be difficult when we disagree with the ruling, yet God clearly has called us to submission in these cases. We honor Him, further the Kingdom and potentially create opportunities to speak God's truth when we are obedient to God.

1. Paul clearly states that believers once were filled with foolishness, disobedience, deception and other ill-fated characteristics. It is only through God's mercy that believers can look forward to eternal life rather than eternal judgment. Because of the mercy extended to you, where can you extend mercy to others as a testimony and sign of God's great love, mercy and grace?

2. Paul called Titus and those Titus led to do good works, not because they were a means to salvation, but because they were the result of salvation already received. What good works is God calling you to do? How can you incorporate good works into your daily efforts as a sign of appreciation for all God has done for you?

PHILEMON

While under house arrest in Rome, Paul met and witnessed to an escaped slave. Once the slave, Onesimus, found freedom in Christ, he had a gripping issue to deal with: his status as a runaway slave. Paul wrote this letter to encourage the master, Philemon, to extend forgiveness to his returning slave, a slave on whom Philemon had the legal right to inflict any punishment including death.

Although this is the shortest of Paul's letters, it serves as a model for requesting and extending forgiveness as well as how the body of Christ is called to be inclusive of all believers on an equal basis. Paul wrote specifically about Onesimus and how he hoped Philemon, as master, would respond. Their relationship bears a resemblance to the relationship all believers have with their *master*. Each was once a slave to sin and has experienced redemption through Christ.

PHILEMON

BACKGROUND

Philemon is mentioned nowhere else in the New Testament, and nothing more is known of him than what is contained in this letter. Apphia is thought to be Philemon's wife and Archippus his son or an elder in the church.

OVERVIEW

Paul's use of the words *beloved* and *fellow worker (laborer)* indicate Philemon was a strong believer and united with Paul in his work.

Paul laid the foundation of his appeal to Philemon by praising him for his fervent faith and love for all believers as well as praying that his faith would continually grow in the knowledge and example of Christ. Philemon's great love was as much an inspiration and source of joy for Paul as it was for those Philemon served.

As a recognized apostle, Paul felt he could command Philemon to do as he requested. Instead, Paul wanted to make his appeal based on the foundational love that existed between the two men as members of the body of Christ.

As he had with his other converts, Paul referred to Onesimus as his son (2 Tim 1.2; Tit. 1.4).

Paul used a play on words when he said Onesimus was now *useful (profitable)* to both Philemon and himself. Onesimus was a common name for slaves because it means *useful*.

Though Onesimus had shown his worth to Paul as a believer, Paul did not want to put him to work in ministry until he had Philemon's permission to do so. Onesimus had not been voluntarily set free by his master and would continue under the cloud of a fugitive slave until his master declared he was free. Paul did not want Philemon to act because he had been commanded but because he voluntarily chose to do so.

Paul referred to Onesimus' new position in Christ and, therefore, brother in Christ to Philemon. This was not equivalent to the temporary position of a slave but was an eternal relationship in Christ.

It is thought that Onesimus stole some property from Philemon when he left. At the very least, Onesimus would owe Philemon for the time he had been absent. Wanting to ensure that nothing would stand in the way of reconciliation between master and slave, Paul offered to clear up any debt Onesimus may have owed. Paul reminded Philemon, however, that he also had a debt to Paul, this one a spiritual debt. Paul did not use this as a leveraging point or an appeal to have the debt cancelled. Rather, he was pointing out the similarities between the two men.

Do even more than I say was a hint at the hope Paul had that Philemon would grant Onesimus his freedom.

Paul had every hope of being released from prison and having the freedom himself to visit Philemon.

Paul's companions are all mentioned in Acts or his letters.

Paul ended his letter as he began it, praying that God's peace would be upon Philemon.

INSIGHTS

Paul's offer to pay Philemon whatever Onesimus owed is a picture of what Christ has done for all who choose to believe in Him. God declared that the penalty for sin is death. He allowed temporary restoration to be made through the Old Testament sacrificial system. Christ came as the perfect sacrifice and permanently paid the penalty on behalf of sinful humanity. Just as Paul had no obligation to pay the debt Onesimus owed, so Jesus had no obligation to pay our debt. Jesus did pay the debt in order to show mercy to us and so that we no longer have a debt before God.

1. Are there people we have some degree of authority over (children, spouse, and subordinates) with whom we might be tempted to use force when an appeal based on Christian love would be more effective?

2. Paul was willing to stand in the gap between Onesimus and Philemon in order to facilitate reconciliation between two believing brothers in Christ. Who might God be calling you to stand in the gap for? How can you serve as a catalyst to reconciliation between those who are feuding?

HEBREWS

The Letter to the Hebrews appears to have been written to address doubts that were cropping up among some believers. The heavy use of Old Testament references and ideas suggests the audience was familiar with Jewish scriptures and practices and therefore Hebrew in nature, though this is uncertain. The author contends that the doubts these believers were dealing with could all be answered by the supremacy and sufficiency of Jesus Christ. S/he focused on three aspects of Christ's life and death: His priesthood, sacrifice and fulfillment of divine promises.

Little is known about who wrote Hebrews. Paul, Silas, Apollos and even Aquila and Priscilla have been suggested as possible authors. While arguments can be made for and against each as well as several others, nothing is known with certainty. Beyond surmising the letter was written to Jewish believers, nothing more is known about the letter's intended audience. The author did not give any indication in the introduction as Paul was accustomed to do, nor are there any clues within the letter.

Hebrews can be divided into three parts. The first focuses on Christ's superiority (1.1-4.13), the second on Jesus Christ as the Great High Priest (4.14-10.18), and the third on living the faith found in Christ (10.19-13.25).

Hebrews, Chapter 1

BACKGROUND

A common practice in ancient Jewish interpretation was the linking of texts by a common word. The writer of Hebrews employs this practice as he cites various Old Testament texts to make his point.

The Septuagint is the Greek translation of the Hebrew Scriptures that was in use at the time Hebrews was written.

OVERVIEW

The author of Hebrews opened by stating in bold and certain terms the place of Christ in the universe. He is the Son of God, the creator and inheritor of all creation and the ultimate means God used to communicate the new covenant with the people He calls to Himself. Having completed the work He was called to do, Christ sits in the place of honor at the right hand of God.

Jesus was not to be thought of as an angel. He sits at the right hand of the God and is therefore of greater rank or honor than the angels.

The author used seven Old Testament references as proof of his claim.

- Ps. 2.7 – originally extolled the Davidic line, however, in this context, *begotten You* likely refers to the completion of the Son's work when He took His rightful place at the right hand of God.

- 2 Sam. 7.14 – linked to the previous text by the word *Son*; a prophecy about the Davidic line and kingdom culminating in the person of Christ.

- Deut. 32.43 – quoted from the Septuagint; angels would worship the One who is over them (firstborn).

- Ps. 104.4 – angels are included in a list of created items that God uses for His purposes.

- Ps. 45.6-7 – Christ is given an eternal throne indicating an eternal reign; *companions* refers to those who will participate in Christ's reign.

- Ps. 102.25-27 – in context, this psalm indicates the *Lord* will come to deliver Israel and the nations; Christ is God in the flesh who will endure forever.

- Ps. 110.1 – only Jesus sits at God's right hand; Jesus himself used this verse as a reference to the Son's presence with the Father (Matt. 22.41-45).

At the time Hebrews was written, some people were tempted to worship angels because they served as God's messengers. The writer used these verses to prove Christ's superiority to angels and His rightful place in the Godhead.

INSIGHTS

As believers raised in a faith that has now existed for 2,000 years, the supremacy of Christ can be taken for granted. Contemplation of this truth can be mind-boggling, awe-inspiring and reassuring all at the same time. God is one God with three distinct persons. Although each of us was created in His image we are separated from Him by sin. Yet He loves us so much that He made the ultimate sacrifice on our behalf by sending His Son to bear our sin. And Jesus, God's very Son, indeed God Himself, walked the earth in human form, died a horrendous death, rose to conquer death and left us with hope that is full of certainty and will not fail.

1. Have you ever stopped to consider precisely what you believe about the Son of God? Does what you believe line up with the opening statements and Old Testament quotes found in Hebrews?

2. Does Jesus receive the attention and reverence He deserves as you go about your day-to-day activities?

Hebrews, Chapter 2

BACKGROUND

The author included five exhortations in his letter: 2.1-4; 3.1-4.16; 5.11-6.20; 10.19-39; 12.1-29⁵.

Qal vahomer or *how much more* was a Jewish form of argument that stated if A (lesser point) is true, how much more is B (greater point) true. The argument doesn't always use the exact wording, but it can generally be recognized by its form. Such an argument appears in 2.1-3.

OVERVIEW

Old Testament passages confirmed the common belief that angels served as God's messengers. Building on the previous chapter in which the writer established Christ's supremacy to the angels, if people heeded the message of angels, so much more should they heed the message of the the Lord—a message confirmed by the workings of God.

The author quoted Ps. 8.4-6 to show that God created humanity to have dominion over all other created things. However, the presence of sin negated God's original plan from taking effect. Jesus' return to rule and reign over the earth will be accompanied by humanity sharing in that rule and returning to their place of dominion.

To emphasize His humanity, the author used the Messiah's human name. Jesus, the God-man, would accomplish what Adam and all humanity had failed to do.

Jesus was not made perfect through His suffering; as God He was already perfect. In contemporary writings, perfect was often used to describe the righteous person whose life ended in martyrdom.

Those who believe in Christ, along with Jesus Himself, all look to God as Father. Therefore believers are called brothers of Christ.

To make his point that believers are brothers of Christ, the author quoted three Old Testament verses. The first, Ps. 22.22 is a messianic psalm in which the Savior associates Himself with those who place their faith in God. The second, Is. 8.17, and third, Is. 8.18, both speak of a prophet who would be rejected and suffer greatly, yet become a focal point for the faithful.

With the relationship between Christ and the believers established, the author pointed out two reasons for this association. First, Christ overcame the power of death and by extension, the Devil. Second, fear of death is one way the Devil holds people in bondage. Christ's victory over death released believers from such enslavement.

Seed of Abraham can refer to either physical or spiritual descendants. In either case, Christ came to free humans, not angels.

Christ came in human form to enable humans to identify with Him as the sympathetic and trustworthy High Priest. The term High Priest is used sixteen times in Hebrews, eleven of those in relation to Christ, who is given the title for the first time in the New Testament. In addition, Christ's suffering allows believers to further identify with Him through their own suffering.

INSIGHTS

The suffering Jesus endured on our behalf releases us from the penalty of death God warned would accompany sin. In addition, Jesus' suffering means there is nothing we endured that He has not also experienced. As a result, we can find peace in the midst of suffering knowing that we are not alone in our agony. Jesus also experienced such agony and, therefore, can extend His mercy, grace, peace, and endurance in just the right way at just the right time. God's love for us knows no end.

1. The author emphasizes Jesus' deity and humanity. Why is it important to recognize that Jesus was both fully human and fully God?

2. How does Jesus' victory over Satan and the power of death free us from the fear of death?

Hebrews, Chapter 3

BACKGROUND

One of the common themes found in the Epistles, including Hebrews, is correcting the false teaching and confusion that constantly tries to enter and destroy true faith. In all cases, the writers, as is especially clear in Hebrews, call the faithful back to scripture and the Holy Spirit as the source of truth. God does not change (Mal. 3.6), and, therefore, neither does His Word. As the writers repeatedly stated, faith in the truth of God is the only assurance of eternal reward.

OVERVIEW

Apostle means *one sent*. It is used only here as a title for Jesus and indicates He was sent by God.

Moses was viewed as one of the great prophets of the Jewish faith and was revered for his obedience to God. *In all his house* alludes to Num. 12.7 and referred to the tabernacle, which Moses faithfully completed according to God's instructions.

Since the author has equated Jesus with God and stated that God built all things, he implies that the new covenant (represented by the house) made as a result of Jesus' death is greater than the covenant made with Moses at Mt. Sinai.

Those who place their faith and confidence in the house (i.e. covenant) Jesus made will experience joy and eternal life.

The author's quote from Ps. 95.7-11 was included as a warning to the readers not to harden their hearts against God. The exodus generation had done so and had suffered as a consequence. God was not beyond disciplining His people again for such behavior.

Rest is a focal point of this chapter and the next. In the Old Testament, rest referred to the time when Israel had ceased fighting and taken possession of the Promised Land (Deut. 3.20; Josh 21.44; 22.4). In the New Testament, rest refers to the eternal life believers will experience as a result of the faith they place in Christ.

God calls all people to believe in Him and the saving work of His Son. Failure to do so is akin to opposing God and anything against God is evil. As a result, an unbelieving heart is evil.

The writer ended the chapter with a series of rhetorical questions designed to reinforce the last point.

INSIGHTS

Each day a person lives is called *today* and represents the time a person has to hear and obey the gospel message. Yesterday cannot be changed and tomorrow may not come. Only today has real value. As believers, each of us is called to make the most of the days we are given. One of the great temptations presented by the world is to focus solely on plans for tomorrow (when the children are grown, graduation, retirement, summer vacation, etc.). The risk of such a focus is missing the opportunities God presents us with today. God will take care of tomorrow for us when we obey Him today (Matt. 6.34).

1. What does it mean to be God's holy people with thoughts fixed on Jesus?

2. How do we guard against having a sinful, unbelieving heart that may turn away from God? What role do other believers have in helping us stay strong?

Hebrews, Chapter 4

BACKGROUND

"Gospel" means *good news*. While the people of Moses' time did not hear the "gospel" in the way the word is used today to mean the message of Christ, they did hear God's *good news* of peace and rest.

OVERVIEW

Building on the warning of the consequences of rebelling against God, the author moves to explaining what *rest* is in this chapter.

The generation Moses led out of Egypt did not *profit* from God's message because they did not put their faith in what they heard.

Some commentators have stated that God's rest lasts through all history because the seventh day of creation did not have an evening (i.e. the day coming to an end; Gen. 2.2).

The author quoted Ps. 95.11 twice in this chapter to emphasize the consequence of not experiencing God's rest as a result of rebelling against God.

Just entering the Promised Land did not bring rest upon God's people. Joshua confirmed this by speaking of a future day in which the rest would be experienced.

The *rest* spoken of in verse 9 is a different Greek word than the other uses of rest and is used only here in the New Testament. Jews taught that the Sabbath foreshadowed eternity. The rest that took place on the Sabbath was a taste of the rest that would be experienced in eternity.

The author warned his readers and himself of the need for continued diligence to avoid falling into disobedience.

When the Day of Judgment comes, God's Word will be the standard against which all are measured. God's Word is not a relic of the past but alive and active in the lives of all people. It has the ability to cut through those things that seem inseparable and has the power to expose that which seems hidden. One day every person will stand in judgment before God and give an account of all they have done, including their thoughts and intents, which can appear to be hidden but are not ever hidden from God.

The high priest was the only person who could enter the most sacred Holy of Holies and then he was permitted to do so only once a year. Jesus, as the greatest of High Priests, not only caused the veil before the Holy of Holies to rip (thereby allowing permanent access to the Father by believers), He also entered heaven to sit at the right hand of the Father.

Jesus, Son of God emphasizes both Jesus' humanity and divinity. Jesus is not a detached deity who does not understand the human plight. Instead, in His humanity, He experienced the same temptations and suffering all people encounter. As a result He is able to sympathize (enter into suffering) with those who are afflicted.

The cumulative result is that believers are now welcomed at the throne of God where they will find compassion and favor in times of need.

INSIGHTS

In the scope of world religions, the various deities are generally far removed and unapproachable by their subjects. Contemplating that with the contrasting intimacy and approachability of God through the work of Christ can be astonishing. For all who believe, Jesus forever removed the barrier that separates humanity from God. Each of us who believes not only may approach the throne but also is welcome there. As believers, we can daily approach the throne through prayer, solitude, studying God's Word, and even fasting and suffering for the gospel.

1. Rest is an important part of God's economy. What is significant about God's promise of rest? How do we experience God's rest in our lives today?

2. What does it mean that Jesus was tempted in every way we are but did not sin? What strength and comfort can we gain from fully appreciating that there is no temptation we face that Jesus did not also face?

Hebrews, Chapter 5

BACKGROUND

The Day of Atonement was the primary focal point during the year. On this day, the high priest made a sacrifice to atone for his sins, and then made another sacrifice to atone for the sins of the people. Blood from each sacrifice was sprinkled on the mercy seat. God called Aaron to be the first high priest (Lev. 16).

Melchizedek was a Canaanite priest-king who blessed Abraham and to whom Abraham paid tithes. Little more is known of him (Gen. 14.18-20).

OVERVIEW

Having introduced Jesus as High Priest in the previous chapter, the author turned to what it means to be a high priest. A high priest was a person appointed by God to represent the people to God. Because he represented the people, the high priest had to identify with their human nature.

The author once again cited Ps. 2.7 to show that Christ had not assumed the position on his own initiative but had been called by God to the position of High Priest. He also cited Ps. 110.4 to show that Christ came from the order of Melchizedek and to highlight the never-ending nature of this priesthood.

Unlike the Old Testament high priests, Jesus did not have to offer a sacrifice for Himself. His offering, made on behalf of all people, consisted of prayers, supplication, cries and tears, as well as His own life.

Jesus did not need to learn to obey in the sense that He was disobedient. In order to fully identify with humanity, Jesus had to live through the experience of obeying God's will. In a similar manner, Jesus was not made perfect because He had previously been imperfect. He was made perfect because He experienced temptation and suffering, yet was perfectly obedient to the will of God. That obedience led to the ultimate cost — death — and resulted in Jesus becoming the source (author) of eternal life.

Dull of hearing means "sluggish" or "apathetic." Though the author's readers had heard God's Word, they had grown lazy in their faith and did not easily understand.

The author said his readers *ought to be teachers* not in the sense that they all had the spiritual gift of teaching but in the sense that they should be mature enough to impart to others what they had learned about the faith.

Milk and *solid food* were common analogies for basic truths and more in depth understanding of truth respectively.

The readers did not necessarily have a lack of information concerning righteousness but a lack of experience in practicing what they knew to be true.

Practice and obedience in the areas of righteousness lead to maturity and an ability to discern or distinguish good from evil.

INSIGHTS

As believers we are called to mature in our faith. This is an active command that requires effort on our part. Such maturity comes from reading and seeking to understand God's word and then applying the truths we learn to our daily lives. Failure to do so will cause us to become *dull* in our faith just as the first century readers had. Though many would disagree, adherence to God's Word frees us from the lies of the enemy and the message of the world that seeks to place us in bondage to great promises that *always* fail to deliver in the end. Only God's Word gives us the freedom and fulfillment we innately long for.

1. What does it mean that Jesus serves as our high priest or representative before God?

2. In the Old Testament, the high priest offered gifts and sacrifices on behalf of the people. Jesus, as the ultimate high priest, made the ultimate sacrifice, His life, for our sins. How can we fully appreciate what Jesus has done for us? How will our relationship with God change as a result?

3. The author stated that distinguishing good from evil was the result of training and maturity. What habits and spiritual practices can you incorporate in your life to ensure you are growing in maturity in Christ?

Hebrews, Chapter 6

BACKGROUND

Laying on of hands was used in both the Old and New Testaments. In the Old it was used to commission a person for service to the Lord (Num. 8.10; 27.18) and when presenting certain sacrificial offerings to the Lord (Lev. 4.4; Num. 8.12). In the New Testament laying on of hands was used to ordain someone for ministry (Acts 6.6; 13.3) and to bestow the Holy Spirit (Acts 8.17; 19.6).

OVERVIEW

As a continuation of the author's encouragement to mature (go on to perfection) in the faith, he suggests his readers move from the basics (called the elementary teachings or principals), six of which he listed. Dead works are those that a person did hoping to earn favor or salvation with God. At the time the author wrote this letter, dead works would have referred to the mandates of the Mosaic Law (the sacrificial system), which had been replaced by the new covenant made by Christ through His death and resurrection.

Baptisms may have referred to the ritual washings performed by the Jewish people or to the various baptisms recorded in the New Testament, such as those called for/performed by John the Baptist or Jesus' and other believers' baptisms.

If God permits is equivalent to "if God wills."

There are several interpretations of the meaning of verses 4-6. Some believe these verses refer to those who nominally believe in Christ and eventually renounce such belief. Others think the author was offering a hypothetical illustration of what would happen to those who refused to mature in the faith. Still others believe the author was referring to those who genuinely accept Christ but later renounce Him.

Jesus would be *crucified again* when a believer who claimed the salvation of Christ later rejected Him. In effect, they were rejoining those who had publicly supported Christ's crucifixion and their rejection amounted to a re-crucifixion.

The author used two illustrations of land that received rain. In one case, the land was productive and thereby useful. In the other, the land was unproductive and rejected. The consequence of being burned is not symbolic of eternal judgment but of the temporal judgment God uses to restore relationship with those who would turn their lives back to Him.

Though much could happen to those who fell away from the faith, the author was confident that better things would occur for his readers. They would experience the rewards of a just God who was well aware of the work they had done and the love they had shown on His behalf.

Though humans will swear by one greater than themselves, there is no one greater than God, so His oaths have been made in His own name (Gen. 22.16).

The confirmation of an oath refers to its function as a guarantee to the agreement reached or the statement made.

The two *immutable (unchanging)* things to which the author referred are God's Word and His promises. These provide the believer with hope; a hope that is found in the certainty and security of the One who can enter into the very presence (behind the veil) of God, namely, Jesus Christ.

INSIGHTS

The author encouraged his readers in the *full assurance of hope*. God through His immeasurable grace and the saving work of His Son loves each of us more than we can ever begin to comprehend. That love provides the basis on which we can hope for the future. In our humanness, we can often have doubts about the reality of our hope, or the extent to which we can have hope. God's promises never fail, nor does His Word; all God has said will come to pass. As we gain confidence in the truth of Heb. 6:11-12, our hope in the future can not only bring us great joy but strong encouragement to do what we are called to do today.

1. Are there any elementary teachings or practices you hold onto but which you have matured past? What intermediate or advanced teachings and practices might God be calling you to?

2. How do God's unchanging word and promises serve as hope in your life? How do they point to the Grace and mercy of God as revealed through Jesus Christ?

HEBREWS, CHAPTER 7

BACKGROUND

Melchizedek is a combination of two Hebrew words: *melek* means "king" and *tzedeq* means "righteousness." Salem means "peace." Melchizedek set the stage for the King who will one day reign in righteousness and as a result bring peace.

Many of the author's arguments presented in this chapter are based on Ps. 110.4.

OVERVIEW

One ancient principle of interpretation held that if a thing was not stated, it did not happen. On this basis, the author can state that Melchizedek was without father, mother or genealogy. The absence of these details in Genesis, a book filled with genealogies, would have been noteworthy to ancient readers. As was the style, the author draws conclusions from the absence of details.

Abraham was the patriarch of the faith, but the author pointed out that there was one greater than Abraham as evidenced by the tithes paid by Abraham to Melchizedek. In addition, Melchizedek represents priesthood without end because Genesis contains no record of his death. The author further pointed out that in a symbolic way the Levitical priests also paid a tithe to Melchizedek. Though Levi and his descendants had not yet been born, they were descendants of Abraham and effectually paid a tithe through their forefather, Abraham.

If the priests who descended from Levi had been able to fully reconcile the people to God, no further priests would have been needed. Since this was not the case, a priest, not of the order of Levi but of the order of Melchizedek, would fill the need.

Since the way to salvation does not ultimately come through the Levitical priests, neither can it come through the Mosaic Law, which they administer.

Jesus, who was of the order of Melchizedek, descended through the non-priestly tribe of Judah.

The superiority of this alternate priesthood is further evident by the oath (as recorded in Ps. 110.4) under which it was established.

The Levitical priesthood, because it consisted of mortal men, needed many priests. The priesthood that would bring salvation would need only one priest because He would live forever, allowing Him to represent all people in all times.

The author concludes with a summary of the superiority of Jesus' priesthood. *Higher than the heavens* means Jesus is esteemed more than any other. Jesus, though fully man, was also fully God, and therefore perfect. As a result, He did not need to offer sacrifices for His own sins. He also did not need to make repeated sacrifices for the sins of the people because the one, perfect, sinless sacrifice of His own life was all that was needed. Finally, Jesus' everlasting appointment by oath is far superior to the weakness of temporal human high priests.

INSIGHTS

The author of Hebrews went to great pains to establish the superiority of Jesus Christ as priest and Savior. In spiritual matters, however, it can be easy to settle for superficial matters rather than focusing on what is most important. Today, many people focus on angels instead of God who created them; they seek truth but fail to seek the One who defines all truth; and they attempt to search for and seek God without ever stopping to realize He has already been pursuing them. Seeking the insignificant, while missing the will of God will result in a disappointing and unfulfilling experience. Only God will satisfy that which we seek.

1. The author states Jesus became high priest not because of his ancestry but because of the power of an indestructible life. What does this mean? Why is it significant?

2. Jesus' priesthood means it is only through Him that anyone can be saved. How does this truth negate the concept that there are many paths leading to heaven?

Hebrews, Chapter 8

BACKGROUND

At the time the letter to the Hebrews was written (likely the late 60s A.D.), the temple in Jerusalem was still functioning. Because of persecution, many Jews were already living outside of Jerusalem. In 70 A.D. the Roman general Titus destroyed the temple to once and for all put down the Jewish uprisings that had been occurring. With the temple destroyed, the sacrificial system of the Mosaic covenant ceased to be practiced, fulfilling the words of the author of Hebrews.

OVERVIEW

The sanctuary in the temple referred to the Holy of Holies, God's dwelling place on earth. The High Priest now ministering in the temple is not limited to the earthly realm. He also ministers in God's presence in heaven in the sanctuary that He Himself built.

The establishment of the temple and priesthood as handed down to Moses on Mt. Sinai was not a new design but served as a shadowy copy of God's heavenly dwelling.

In His position, Jesus provides a better ministry, covenant and promise than the earthly replicas were able to impart.

Although not the first covenant made, the author used *first covenant* to refer to the one consisting of the Mosaic Law.

The author quoted Jer. 31.31-34 to show that even in the Old Testament the first covenant was recognized as insufficient and would be replaced by a second, better covenant.

According to Jeremiah four terms would be included in the new covenant:

- God's laws will be written on people's hearts instead of stone tablets.

- God will have a relationship with believers.

- Mediators such as priests or Pharisees will no longer be needed; God will make Himself known directly to all people.

- God will display His mercy by forgiving sins and remembering them no longer.

With the establishment of the second covenant, the first would become obsolete and cease to be practiced.

INSIGHTS

The four terms of the new covenant are worth contemplating. The God of the Universe desires to have a personal relationship with every person who places his or her faith in Him and the saving work of His Son. In order to have such a relationship, God has removed the need for mediators. We can approach Him (through prayer, study of His Word, meditation, etc.) directly. In addition, He readily forgives us our sins and ceases to remember them (hold them against us) any longer (Ps 103.12). Once forgiven, we need never worry or feel guilty about what we have done in the past. (This doesn't remove the consequences but does cleanse us from the wrongdoing.)

1. Both the covenants given to Moses and through Jesus include tabernacles, high priests and sacrifices. What are the similarities and differences of each of these as they relate to the old and new covenants?

2. The author's lengthy quote of Jeremiah includes four terms that would be included in the new covenant. How are those terms evident in Christians today? Is each term a part of your Christian experience?

HEBREWS, CHAPTER 9

BACKGROUND

The three items placed inside the Ark of the Covenant served as symbols of the Mosaic covenant and reminders of God's presence with and provision for His people. The pot of manna reminded the people of God's care and provision while they wandered in the desert. Aaron's rod symbolized the priestly authority God bestowed on Aaron and his descendants as they served as God's representatives to the people. The tablets were the Ten Commandments and represented God's care for His people through the Law.

OVERVIEW

The author described the sanctuary with some detail. He followed the layout outlined in the Old Testament fairly specifically, though it is known that the temple of the then contemporary times was somewhat different.

Though the author indicates the censor was inside the Most Holy Place, it was actually kept just outside the dividing veil. Its use is most closely associated with the Most Holy Place and this provides the likely reason for the apparent placement within the Most Holy Place.

The priests performed regular rituals in the Holy Place including burning incense twice a day and changing the showbread every Sabbath. The Most Holy Place, on the other hand, was entered only once a year on the Day of Atonement and only by the high priest.

The limited access to the Most Holy Place by just one person pointed to the inadequacy of the Mosaic covenant to fully reconcile the people to God. It was symbolic of the covenant that would be established but served only a temporary purpose until that time.

The sacrificial offerings the human priests made had only a temporary and limited ability to bring redemption to the people. On the other hand, Christ's sacrificial offering of His own, spotless blood provided eternal redemption and no further sacrifice was needed.

The sacrifices made with human hands had the ability to cleanse on an external basis only; they could not cleanse the heart. Christ's sacrifice went far deeper and was able to cleanse people internally where the defilement actually took place.

The author encouraged his readers to set aside adherence to the Mosaic covenant, which was filled with dead works that could not bring salvation and instead grasp the eternal cleansing of Christ.

Two gifts are given through the new covenant: redemption and inheritance.

Depending on the translation, the Greek word translated as *covenant* in verse 15 is translated as *will*, *testament*, or *covenant* in verse 16. A will is a legal document that takes effect after someone has died. Though the Mosaic covenant was ratified by blood, it was not the blood of someone who had died.

If the copies required blood to be ratified, then so did the *heavenly* covenant.

Christ is able to enter the true sanctuary and did not have to enter the copy made by human hands. In addition, He did not have to offer regular sacrifices. Instead, He offered one that satisfied the penalty for all people over all time.

Christ's one time sacrifice will be followed by His second appearance, which is not to fulfill the penalty for sin as the first one was, but to deliver the final judgment—allowing all those who believe to experience eternal life while those who do not believe will be sent to eternal death.

INSIGHTS

The author of Hebrews called Christ a mediator. In this position, He brought about reconciliation between two parties – God and humanity – who had been divided by humanity's choice to sin. Unlike most mediators, Christ performed the deed required to bring that reconciliation to pass. In addition, Christ also stands before the Father as an advocate for all who place their trust in Him. In this role, Christ pleads the worthiness of believers before the Father and covers the required penalty with His own blood offering. Not only do believers have the opportunity to stand before the Father, they do so with no penalty to pay.

1. The three items placed in the ark of the covenant – manna, Aaron's staff and the stone tablets – served as reminders. What were they to remind the people of? While these were part of the now obsolete old covenant, they can still serve as reminders today. What aspects of God's character do these items point to?

2. Why is it significant that Jesus entered the Most Holy Place (Holy of Holies) by His own blood rather than as the priests of old entered by the blood of animal sacrifices?

BACKGROUND

Old Testament law differentiated between unintentional and intentional sin (Num. 15.29-31). Intentional sins were those that blatantly and willfully rejected God. The sacrificial system was designed to atone for unintentional sin. No sacrifice was prescribed for intentional sin. Instead, a person was to be completely cut off from the community and was responsible for bearing his/her own guilt.

OVERVIEW

The author continued on the theme of the inadequacy of the sacrifices offered under the Mosaic covenant. Had those sacrifices been sufficient to remove sin, they would have not have been continually offered. The blood of those sacrifices could not completely atone for sin and, therefore, served as a reminder of the sin that had occurred.

The author quoted Ps. 40.6-8, indicating it was a messianic prophecy that could only be filled by Jesus and not David. Obedience as well as sacrifice was required by God to atone for sins. The psalm indicates that Jesus' obedience was one aspect that made His sacrifice better than those offered under the Mosaic covenant.

From the quote, the author concludes that God abolished (took away) the first (Mosaic) covenant so that He might establish the second, better covenant made through Christ's obedient sacrifice.

Priests always stood in the sanctuary because there was always a sacrifice to offer. In contrast, Christ made His one, perfect sacrifice and sat down in the sanctuary, waiting for His enemies to be made His footstool. The act of sitting down indicates Christ accomplished what He set out to do; His work was done.

Since Christ's perfect sacrifice redeemed believer's sin once and for all, there is no need for God to remember the sins and no need for any further sacrifice.

Christ's redeeming and restoring sacrifice allows believers to enter the once restricted sanctuary with boldness and come into the very presence of God.

The author gave three commands, each introduced by *let us*. First, believers are to draw near to God in faith that is full of certainty. Just as priests washed before entering the sanctuary, so believers have been washed as with the purest of waters by the shed blood of Christ. Second, believers are to hold fast to the hope their confession of faith provides. Finally, believers are to consider (observe, contemplate) those around them in order to find ways (stir up, spur) to extend love and good deeds to others.

The Hebrew word translated *assembling (meeting)* is a compound form of the word *synagogue*. The author called on his readers to continue gathering in church so they could exhort and encourage one another.

To sin willfully was a conscious act of rejecting God. By extension this means to reject the means of reconciling one's relationship with God and leaves the individual open to God's full wrath and judgment.

With the testimony of two witnesses the penalty for idolatry was death by stoning. The author states that rejecting the work of Christ can only bring worse judgment.

The author encouraged the readers by reminding them of the persecution they endured when they first became believers. Great reward awaited those who did not draw back but remained faithful to Christ.

INSIGHTS

The author's call to continue meeting in church is just as relevant today as it was when written. It can be easy to fall prey to the idea that church is supposed to feed us so we leave satisfied. In reality, church is a place for believers to gather in order to encourage and exhort one another. When we settle for nothing more than what we *get* from church, we abdicate our own responsibility to do the things that cause us to mature in faith and shift the responsibility to the church. It then becomes easy to move from church to church in search of where we *get* the most. Instead, we should focus on what we can give to the body of Christ.

1. The author states that believers have had their hearts sprinkled to cleanse them from a guilty conscience (10.22). What does this say about shame and guilt you may feel about your past? If you continue to carry shame and guilt, what does this say about your understanding of what Jesus has done on the cross? Do you need to change anything in order to fully experience cleansing?

2. The readers of Hebrews were encouraged not to throw away their confidence. How much confidence do you have in what Jesus has done for you? If your confidence needs a boost, what can you do to gain the certainty and conviction needed? How can your confidence serve as a tool in God's hands to further His purposes and plans?

Hebrews, Chapter 11

BACKGROUND

The author noted that Abraham's descendants were *as numerous as the stars in the sky* and as *countless as the sand on the seashore.* Initially, this comparison was thought to be ridiculous as the grains of sand clearly outnumbered the stars in the sky. Recent advances in astrophysics, however, have proven the legitimacy of the comparison.[5]

OVERVIEW

Having concluded his exhortation to live by faith, the author gave a number of examples of Old Testament characters who used their faith to trust in God.

The author begins by describing faith. It is the *reality* that currently does not exist but is hoped for. In addition, it serves as proof for the things that are unseen. For the ancient peoples, particularly the Greeks, those things not seen were eternal things, such as the heavens. Faith allows believers to believe that God created the visible universe out of substance that is not visible.

Seventeen times the author introduces the exhibition of faith by an Old Testament character with the words *by faith.*

Though the Old Testament offers no explanation as to why Abel's sacrifice was accepted while Cain's was not, the author suggests it was because Abel offered his with faith, while Cain lacked faith (Gen. 4.1-5).

[5] Earl Radmacher, Ronald B. Allen, and H. Wayne House, editors, *Nelson's New Illustrated Bible Commentary* (Nashville: Thomas Nelson Publishers), 1655

Enoch was rewarded because of his faith in a God he could not see (Gen. 5.21-24).

Noah's faith resulted in his obedience to do as God commanded even though he could not see the flood that was coming (Gen. 6-9).

Likewise, when Abraham was called to leave his home, his faith caused him to obey (Gen. 12.1-8).

Genesis does not explicitly mention the role Sarah's faith played in her ability to bear her son. The author states that her faith did, in fact, play a role and she bore a son as a result of her faith in God's ability to do the impossible (Gen. 21.2).

Abraham, Sarah and their immediate descendants (Isaac and Jacob) could have returned to the native land of Ur had they chosen. Instead, they had faith in God and stayed where He called them.

Isaac, Jacob and Joseph each believed until the end of their lives and passed that belief on to the generations that followed through blessings and instructions (Gen. 27.19-29; 49.1-20; 50.24-26).

Moses' parents showed faith by hiding their son (Ex. 2.1-10).

Moses himself showed faith by repeatedly obeying God. (Ex. 2.11-14.23).

The Israelites experienced their first victory in the Promised Land when they had faith in God's unconventional method of defeating Jericho (Josh. 6.1-21).

Rahab, the only non-Israelite mentioned in this list, had faith in a God she had only heard about (Josh. 2; 6.22-25).

The author stated he could continue giving examples but would refrain. In doing so, however, he listed several people he could mention as well as some of the exploits that showed their faith. He also pointed out that well placed faith in God did not always result in a peaceful life. Some suffered greatly for their faith. Some of the torturous experiences listed refer to the Maccabean period and the series of rulers who governed Jerusalem and rebelled against Rome.

Made perfect refers to the completed work of salvation when all believers would be raised from the dead.

INSIGHTS

By faith God's people were drawn to Him and responded with obedience to do His will. Today, we too are drawn to God *by faith*. Though we can see evidence of God all around us, we cannot actually see God. It is by faith that we place our trust in Him and in the promises He has made. Many argue that they could never place their faith in something they cannot see. In reality, they do it everyday. Each breath we take is drawn by faith. Each profession of love is made and received by faith. Though God walks with us daily, the greatest result of our belief in Him by faith is the eternal life we will one day enjoy.

1. This chapter is often referred to as the Hall of Faith. Why does God require His people to have such faith in Him rather than simply making everything clear? How does God use even the smallest amount of faith to serve His purposes? How is God using your faith in Him to minister to the people around you?

2. Many people lived their entire lives without seeing the culmination of God's promises during their lifetimes. Some even suffered persecution because of their faith. How does their example help you stand firm in your faith during times of trial, suffering, and persecution?

HEBREWS, CHAPTER 12

BACKGROUND

The mountain that may be touched referred to Mt. Sinai when God was giving the law to Moses. The people were so afraid of God's voice that they wanted Moses to mediate between them and God (Ex. 20.18-21).

OVERVIEW

Cloud was a figurative term that was often applied to a crowd. The witnesses were the faithful mentioned in the previous chapter. *Weight* refers to anything that would slow a runner down and is used to denote anything that would keep the reader from living a life of faith.

Using a racing analogy, the author called his readers to model the faith of the witnesses and finish the race of faith set before them—a race that Christ had already run and for which he had done everything necessary for believers to finish.

Christ is to serve as the example for all those who grow weary in their own faith.

Though Christ's suffering had ultimately resulted in His death, the reader's suffering had not yet reached a similar level of persecution.

The author quoted Prov. 3.11-12 to show that God uses discipline to admonish and correct the behavior of those He loves, just as a father disciplines his own son because of love. In this context, such discipline includes persecution.

In ancient Roman society, illegitimate sons received very little recognition from their fathers and had no rights of inheritance. Those who did not receive correction from God were akin to illegitimate sons and would not receive the promised inheritance. As a result, believers should readily welcome God's discipline.

God's discipline is done with divine wisdom and is solely for the believer's own good. Its ultimate goal is to mold believers into the likeness and image of Christ that they might also share in His holiness.

Make a straight path likely refers to finding the quickest route in a long distance race.

Experiencing God's presence is realized only by seeking peace and holiness. The readers were warned to be on guard for three dangers: falling short of God's grace resulted when someone rejected the salvation found in Christ, bitterness taking root when believers failed to forgive those who offended them, and valuing sexual temptation, food or anything else over God.

In contrast to the law given on Mt. Sinai, believers are now called to a heavenly Jerusalem on Mt. Zion, attended by angels and believers—the place where the new covenant was established by Christ's blood.

The author encouraged his readers not to reject the salvation offered by Christ. Christ warned people when He was on earth. Now that He is in heaven, those who still see fit to reject Him will suffer great condemnation.

The author quoted Hag. 2.6 to indicate the judgment of God from which nothing would escape. He used Deut. 4.24 as a reminder for those who might abandon the faith that such action would not be without consequences.

INSIGHTS

A kingdom that cannot be shaken reflects the author's confidence in God, the saving work of Christ and the victory that has already been realized in the battle over evil. In our everyday lives, it can be easy to lose sight of this victory. By remembering the victory and living in confidence that it has occurred, we can gain greater peace, boldness and conviction. Though Christ has not yet returned the second time to establish His kingdom on earth, God has already achieved victory over Satan. Trusting in God and all His promises is to choose the winning side!

1. What is your view of discipline? As you experience God's discipline, how is it a sign of His great love for and mercy toward you? God's discipline can be difficult and embarrassing to endure. How can you embrace God's discipline so that you grow in faith and maturity?

2. The author encouraged his readers to make every effort to live in peace, to be holy, to look for God's grace, and to avoid bitterness. Do you practice these in your day-to-day life? Are there any spiritual practices or other items you can add to your daily life to better embrace the author's suggestion?

Hebrews, Chapter 13

BACKGROUND

Perhaps the most well known occurrence of hosting visitors who turned out to be angels was done by Abraham when he was told Sarah would have a child (Gen. 18.1-14).

In Roman times, prisons most often served more as detention centers than actual places of punishment. Prisoners would be kept in prison until their trial. If a prisoner was found guilty, a punishment was pronounced and carried out. While awaiting trial, prisoners sometimes had to depend on family and friends for their food and clothing, which often were not provided by the government.

OVERVIEW

The author closed his letter with a series of instructions on how to live the faith in practical ways.

The prisoners the author exhorted the readers to remember were likely believers who were being persecuted for their faith. *In the body* was a reference to the readers' physical bodies. They were at risk of suffering persecution as long as they were alive.

Fornicators referred to anyone who engaged in sexual activity outside of marriage, including heterosexual and homosexual relations. Adulterers referred to anyone who was unfaithful to his/her spouse.

The command not to covet is covered by the last of the Ten Commandments. Those who were obedient to God could count on His presence and provision in their lives. The author quoted Josh. 1.5 and Ps. 118.6 to make his point.

The exhortation to *remember those who rule over you* is thought to mean Christian leaders who had died. Their example was worthy of following.

Strange doctrines referred to those contrary to the gospel message. In the context of Hebrews, this would include primarily the Jewish ritual observances that Jewish religious leaders alleged were necessary to gain entrance into heaven.

On the Day of Atonement, the high priest made a sacrifice to atone for the sins of the people. It was burned outside the city and the high priest was not permitted to eat a portion of it as was permitted for other sacrifices made throughout the year.

Being outside the gate (of the city) was considered dangerous and for Jews symbolized separation from the community. The author called those who believed in Jesus to follow Him outside the gate. In effect he was calling his readers to abandon Judaism and proclaim the good news of Christ.

The new Jerusalem is yet to come. As a result, believers do not have a permanent home on earth but await their home to come with eternal life.

The animal sacrifices that are no longer valid or needed can be replaced with spiritual sacrifices of praise.

Believers should submit to the authority of those who rule over them for they will one day be held accountable for their actions.

Being held a prisoner, which was preventing Him from visiting those to whom he wrote, may have motivated the author's request for prayer.

Each of the six times *God of peace* is used in the New Testament (Rom. 15.33; 1 Cor. 14.33; 2 Cor. 13.11; Phil 4.9; 1 Thess. 5.23; Heb. 13.20), it is used because the recipients were experiencing some sort of trial or difficulty. The readers of this letter were contemplating returning to Judaism due to the persecution they were suffering.

The author prayed that his readers would be open to the workings of God, that His will might be fulfilled through the service (good works) they performed.

INSIGHTS

For the early believers, praising God in a Christian rather than Jewish way could result in persecution, loss of property and even loss of life. Today, we don't often think of our praises to God as a sacrifice, yet they can be when we stand up for what is right instead of succumbing to peer pressure; when we make God a priority instead of using our time and money for our own personal pleasure, and when we follow God even at the cost of family relationships and friendships. Christ gave the ultimate sacrifice for us through His sin atoning death. We can sacrifice to God through our praises in all things.

1. How does visualizing yourself in the shoes of a prisoner or the mistreated help you better minister to and serve those who are suffering?

2. Jesus Christ is the same yesterday, today, and forever. How can this truth help you from being influenced by those who desire to lead you astray with half-truths and lies?

Acknowledgements

There are an amazing number of people involved in a project like this. First, my thanks go to Dave Wood for asking me to write a series of New and Old Testament notes to accompany our church's Bible reading program. Dave saw something in me I did not see. As a result I had the privilege and blessing of seeing God's hand work in and through me in most unexpected ways.

Thanks also go to the leadership and staff of Grace Community Church, in particular Bryan Hochhalter, Doug Kempton, Bryce Gray, Paula Smith, Tracey Krusz and others who worked behind the scenes.

Thank you to Eddie Jones and Lighthouse Publishing of the Carolinas. Eddie's vision for my manuscript and belief in what I had written has been an enormous encouragement and beyond that, has resulted in a published work – a dream come true!

Thank you to Meaghan Burnett who walked me through the entire publication process. I've had to step way out of my comfort zone in some areas. Thank you for your patience, explanations, training and efforts on my behalf.

A myriad of people helped with readying the manuscript for publication. These include Peggy Bennett, Stacey and Martin Bilderbeck, Heather Brdak, Kristine Bresser, Vito Ciaravino, Luke Elliott, Dick Klemisch, Diane Matous, Jennifer Matous, Tom Reisner, Karen Straetmans, Dawn Taylor, and Ally Turner. Thank you for the gift of your time and effort. I appreciate each of you immensely.

With so many people involved right up to the day the books are printed, I am sure I have overlooked someone who rightly deserves to be listed here. Please know this is an oversight. My gratitude goes to you as well!

I could not have finished this project without my husband, Phil. His love, support, encouragement and belief in me have been amazing. More than once I have been overwhelmed with the amount of work needed to complete this series. Each time Phil has reminded me of who I am, whose I am, and the real Author and Finisher of this work. I love you!!

Finally and most importantly, thank you God! You have shown me incredible grace and mercy, gifted me in ways I never would have guessed, been gentle in Your rebukes and showered me with Your blessings. Praise be to You, God our Father and our Lord Jesus Christ!!

Made in the USA
Coppell, TX
09 February 2020